How to Dismantle a Dictatorship

HEATHER MARSH

With grateful appreciation to my patrons and a special thank you for the support of:

Adam Kendall

Douglas Lucas

Fallon Williams

S. Last

Dr. Karen Monroy

Join the Binding Chaos community!

www.mustread.press

www.mustread.press

Copyright © 2025

Heather Marsh

Must
Read

Author photograph by Tryston Powers

Book cover, layout and

illustrations by Ossiel Romero

Ebook: 978-1-989783-39-9
Paperback: 978-1-989783-40-5
Hardcover: 978-1-989783-41-2

Table of Contents

The structure of power..1

Step 1: Remove their identity.............................7

Step 2: Reject their reality.................................25

Step 3: Resist their will.....................................43

Step 4: Block validation....................................61

Step 5: Assign guilt..81

Step 6: Protect the vulnerable..........................97

Step 7: Cultivate external allies......................117

Step 8: Take the focus......................................133

Step 9: Create the alternative.........................145

Afterword...163

The structure of power

Have you ever watched the rise of a tyrant in disbelief that so many people could be bent to the will of so few? Why are tyrants so very difficult to resist? It is because a tyrant is not just a tyrant: it is a tyranny. Imagine a person that no one had ever heard of suddenly demanding that people be arrested and executed, ordering the military to go to war, and changing the structure of government. It would be laughable. One tyrant is not a tyranny. Even a large group of tyrants is not a tyranny.

A tyranny is a change in the nature of a social group. People are changed from acting and being perceived as individuals to acting and being perceived as assigned roles within the structure of power. Their wills are coerced to do another's bidding. Their reality is altered until they believe what they formerly knew were lies. A tyranny changes everyone in the society. To overthrow a tyrant, the whole society must undo the change. This book describes how dictatorships are created and how they can be destroyed.

A dictatorship follows the structure of power. Power is accumulated through the creation of emergency social defence structures. I described these structures, which I call *endogroups*, in *The Creation of Me, Them and Us*. It is very much a part of human nature, and the nature of other social animals, to create such social structures in times of existential threat. When these emergency structures seek to remain permanent, we have an endogroup. An endogroup may appear as abusive relationships in groups of two or more people, and they can scale all the way up to include almost the entire world. At the level of a state, strong endogroups appear in the form of dictatorships. To remove a dictatorship, this structure must first be dismantled.

The endogroup power structure is illustrated in the next diagram.

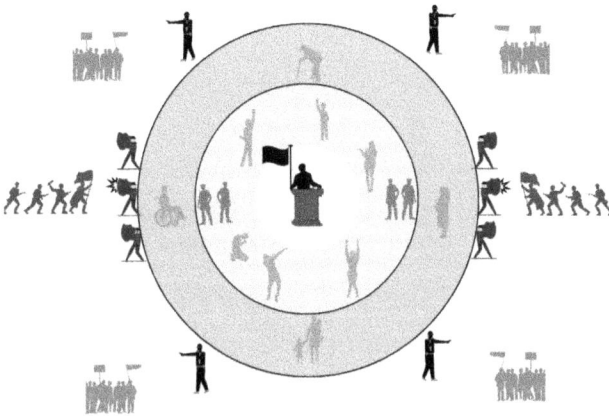

There are six components to every endogroup:

An identity which enables exclusive membership.

An exceptional myth justifying unequal entitlement.

An existential threat from external forces.

An idealized source of collective reality, the endo-ideal, residing in a person or ideology.

A negative image, made up of people identified as opposite the ideal.

Reflectors which may exist separately from the negative image in groups of more than two.

How To Dismantle a Dictatorship

A dictatorship is formed by assembling and strengthening these components. We can reverse engineer an endogroup by removing and weakening each component that holds it together. As each element is removed or disabled, the structure of power will start to crumble. Without the structure, a dictatorship is just one or a few people facing the entire population.

It is important to note that all states are endogroups of varying strengths. This means that all of the strategies in this book to take down a dictatorship can and are used by external enemies as well, to weaken rival states and governments. The goal of this book is to remove a dictatorship but leave the state intact. I will point out examples of hostile use of these techniques to collapse a state and defensive strategies against this as we go.

To keep this book short and easy to read, I will focus on how dictatorships work, not why they work that way. I will explain how to assign guilt, counter the collectively enforced version of reality (*endoreality*) and help move people away from their endogroup roles because that is how to dismantle a dictatorship. I do not explain why endoreality and guilt are so powerful or what they are in a physical sense. Neither do I go into exhaustive detail about the nature and behaviour of endogroups, or why we become locked into roles within a power structure. Finally, I do not discuss global alternatives to states or alternative methods of governance, even though, as endogroups, all states are vulnerable to escalating power. That discussion is relevant, but beyond the scope of fighting a dictator from within one state today.

All of this supporting and adjunct material can be found in the *Binding Chaos* series. There, these aspects are explored in much more detail and discussed in the context of interdisciplinary research, along with ideas for future evolution. Here, we have a concise nine point action list for dismantling a dictatorship, within the current global political framework.

Most people can see that dictators are not extraordinary people in any way, yet they are credited with single-handedly assembling and upholding tyrannies. In reality, the way to topple a dictator is found within ourselves. All dictators are a creation of those who uphold them and those who fail to resist them. People holding or trying to seize power have learned tricks to help them manipulate the public, but once we understand what is happening, we can dismantle power far more easily than it can be accumulated. We have more control because it is happening within us and to us.

Dismantling a dictatorship is not easy, but it is a lot easier than holding one together.

Step 1: Remove their identity

A A king with no subjects is not a king, and a dictator with no state is not a dictator. A dictator is elevated through the creation of a group self, or endogroup. Within this group, each person is assigned a role: *endo-ideal*, *reflector* or *negative image*. The endo-ideal is the idealized self of an endogroup, embodying all virtue, ownership, victimhood and credit in the group. The reflectors uphold and defend the endo-ideal. The negative image acts as the inverse of the endo-ideal and embodies all vice, guilt and shame assigned within the group. Anyone not in the endogroup is a rival outsider.

These roles support the dictatorship: the reflectors legitimize the dictator as their endo-ideal, the negative image shields the dictator by absorbing blame for their actions, and outsiders are excluded as external threats. No one can become an endo-ideal by themselves. There must be public recognition and acceptance of their role and of the supporting roles. Once the endo-ideal is chosen, all empathy, interest and focus of the group will vector towards the endo-ideal. This focus is what solidifies the roles and leads to the accumulation of power.

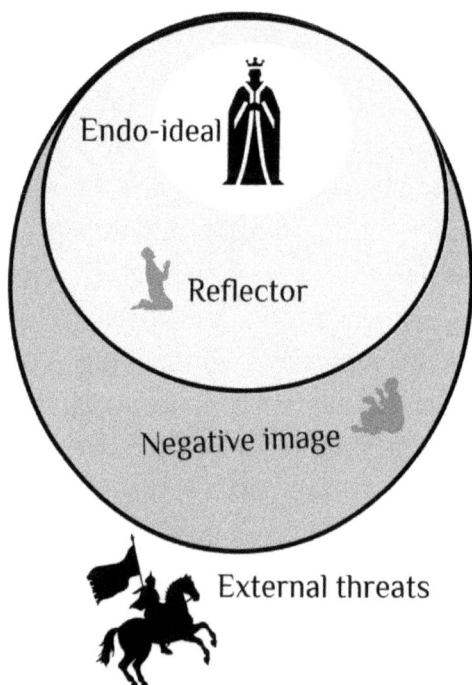

The *endo-identity* is a word used to enable exclusive membership, set an endogroup off as exceptional and create or highlight difference. A state citizenship or nationality is a good example of this. The United States started out with no clear endo-identity, either before or after it gained independence. The area was originally known outside of indigenous nations as separate parts of the British Colonies. This encouraged regional bonding, not collective. During the war for independence, these areas were referred to collectively as the Thirteen Colonies. There were several replacement names floated after independence. The name Columbia was once the favoured choice, hence the name of the new capital, the District of Columbia. This name was nearly identical to Gran Colombia in the south and British Columbia in the north, and it was superseded by an even more generic term, the United States. Many states, including their closest neighbour, the United States of Mexico, also had United States as part of their names.

It wasn't until the very imperialist president, Teddy Roosevelt, that he and the rest of the country began calling themselves *America*. This identity renounced any attempts at cohesive, national uniqueness to reflect imperial ambitions right in the name. Naming a country, family or person as the thing they want to become represents manifest destiny ambitions. This has apparently never ceased going to the heads of US despots since they are still trying to annex other parts of America.

Names which include claims to power are part of an *exceptional myth.* The exceptional myth is the story used to justify unequal entitlement for the endogroup or the endo-ideal. The five types of exceptional myth address superiority, leaders, destiny, creation and persecution. These myths claim superiority through inherent attributes like family or race, great achievements, brilliant leaders, aspirational destiny, divine creation, unprecedented victimhood or a combination of all of these. If all of these myths fail, the endo-ideal are depicted as the lesser evil. In this scenario, they are presented as the sole barrier standing in the way of something much worse, usually an external threat or rival endo-ideal.

A.E.I.O.U., is a motto used by the European imperial family, the Habsburgs, since the 1400s. At the time of its origin, the motto was translated to *all the world is subject to Austria*, Austria at this point being the House of Habsburg. This exceptional myth embodies the entitlement that brought the House, from its founding in the 11th century to the last abdication in 1919, to oversee a vast collection of kingdoms and other holdings, the Holy Roman Empire, the Austrian Empire, and one, brief, Empire of Mexico. It is a myth of divine destiny, similar to others used by most dynasties and empires.

The exceptional myth encourages unjustified glorification of the endo-ideal and unjustified demonization of the negative image, any opposition, or anyone outside the endogroup. The myth is used to forestall any challenge or attempt to assign guilt to the endo-ideal and to cast all opponents as the negative image. If anyone challenges a dictator, the myth is invoked to accuse the challenger of sabotaging the great destiny, challenging the exceptional brilliance, or compounding the unprecedented victimhood of the endo-ideal.

We can see all of these defences at work in the world. People challenging a billionaire are derided as not being worthy to challenge someone so evidently far above them or being jealous. Resistance to atrocities by a state is depicted as a wish for the vilified enemies of the state to succeed. Criticism of corporations is held to be standing in the way of progress. This type of defence is based on the exceptional myth.

There are two ways to depose a tyranny. One is to challenge the entire structure of power, including endo-identities and the exceptional myth. Separatist groups often use this method to challenge a state's authority over a specific region, especially in former empires like Russia and China which govern large and diverse populations, or in formerly colonized countries. It is also a common method for those who want increased autonomy under the protection of the state umbrella, and has been used to challenge state authority by indigenous and quasi-separatist groups worldwide.

The renaming of the First Nations of Canada is an example of such a challenge. This grouping of nations was originally saddled with the name *Indians*, which is an example of *negative image melding* we will get to in *Step 6*. This name served to separate a group of Indigenous people from Inuit, Métis, and everyone else in Canada, who were referred to simply as *Canadians*. First Nations, the replacement name chosen for collective identity, reflects an endo-ideal rightful ownership claim right in the name. A parallel word sometimes presented to refer to all non-indigenous people in Canada is *settler*. This is another negative image melding, which also assigns guilt, a strategy we will explore in *Step 5*.

Unlike the word *Canadians*, which implies rightful ownership of Canada, the word *settler* discredits ownership claims.

These two renamings were very powerful in establishing a claim for legitimacy and precedence in Canadian governance. Such renaming will not dismantle a power structure, but it will challenge the allocation of power within it, by reversing the endo-ideal claim to ownership and adding a negative image assignment of guilt. The use of these two terms became popular at the end of the last century, when treaty rights were a particularly heated struggle in Canada. Today, everyone I know or listen to refers to themselves and others as members of a specific nation(s), and I haven't heard the term *settler* in Canada since the turn of the century.

Challenging state authority through attacks on identity and the exceptional myth has been dangerous for non-separatist resistance since the *Treaties of Westphalia* codified the principle of state sovereignty in 1648. States are endogroups. Dismantling all endogroup trappings means dismantling the state itself. This method is, therefore, used by external enemies of a state so that the state's existence can be denied, and it can be taken over by another. The (supposed) lack of a state endogroup was used to justify conquest of indigenous people worldwide. Russian and US propagandists are currently pushing the idea that Canada and Greenland were not constituted legitimately to justify their annexation. The same method has been used against Ukraine, Palestine and many other states. States are either depicted as lacking historical legitimacy, or they are attacked, weakened, and then pronounced as *failed states*. These tactics can undermine both international support and internal cohesion.

Those who want to keep the state and only rid themselves of the dictatorship cannot dismantle the entire structure of power. In fact, most revolutions strengthen it. All endogroups are strengthened during conflict and events triggering shared pride, so removing a dictator can act as a trigger for extreme nationalism. We will address that in the last chapter, but right now, the best idea for those who wish the state to continue is to not attack the state's identity or validity.

The alternative is to identify the dictator and their dedicated reflectors as a separate endogroup. Russians who refer to Putinists as *Muscovites* and those in the US referring to Trump supporters as *MAGA* are doing just that.

This makes it possible to challenge the dictatorship's legitimacy but not the state's. The use of MAGA is particularly inspired as anyone can refuse the identity and step away from being a Trump reflector. That would not be as simple if the word was something regional like Muscovites or an established political party like Republican.

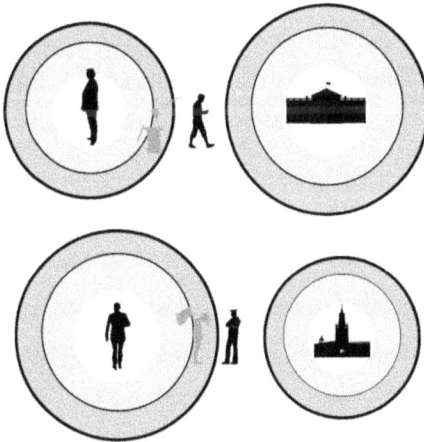

The side which successfully claims the state identity will have a definite advantage. They will present themselves as the legitimate holders of power to external parties. They will, by default, be able to claim the allegiance of uncommitted citizens. If neither group successfully claims the state identity, both sides will have to differentiate themselves and attract the intentional allegiance of each supporter. External observers may be confused as to which group to recognize. This happens sometimes when a transcendental state such as Yugoslavia or the USSR collapses, and both the central and breakaway groups have to define themselves as 'legitimate' states, both externally and internally.

Since you are trying to remove a dictator, you probably have the disadvantage. This is the first thing you should try to turn around. Do not, under any circumstances, identify yourselves as a rival political party, a rebellion, or any new and unknown group. Identify as the people of the state. *Self determination* is recognized as an international legal right in the *UN Charter*. Under the democratic principle of *popular sovereignty*, the people of the state have the authority to reject and replace their ruler. If you are referred to as *the people*, then your movement is more easily accepted as the *general will*, reflecting the *consent of the governed*, and the dictatorship is more clearly seen as an illegitimate, occupying force.

In 1940, the French resistance formed a government in exile led by General Charles de Gaulle, and called it the Free French movement. The Nazi puppet government in power was widely referred to as *the Vichy government*. In

2011, Syrian rebels identified themselves as the Free Syria movement and used the flag Syria used immediately after independence, before the Assad tyranny. They identified Assad and the government flag as *the Ba'athist regime.* However you do it, use the name and the flag which presents you as the legitimate representative of the people.

Dictatorships use the state identity, anthem and flag in great excess in an attempt to appear legitimate and block any other claimants. Take the identity and patriotic trappings from them. Make your identity an idealized vision of the state without the dictator. Create songs and symbols that represent this idealized vision.

As mentioned earlier, every state is an endogroup, and as I have written in the *Binding Chaos* series, we can create much better ways of governing ourselves. Often, resistance movements are justly wary of patriotic trappings and nationalism because they are tools of the oppressor. They may also be very critical of the state and even the people in it. Unfortunately, from the perspective of the endogroup, this serves to identify them as either a rival endogroup or the negative image of the state. Neither identification will win large-scale support from those committed to the endogroup.

To dismantle a dictatorship, you cannot accept an identity as the negative image of the state. That will pit you against the entire endogroup. Violence against you will be viewed as oppression of the negative image and therefore, justified. This violence is a feature of every endogroup and is ignored both externally and internally. If people can look at oppression and say, it is only oppression of women, immigrants, elders, the poor, the sick, or regional outcasts, few will rise up against it. These are negative image categories that most, or all, countries oppress, and people rarely have revolutions about it.

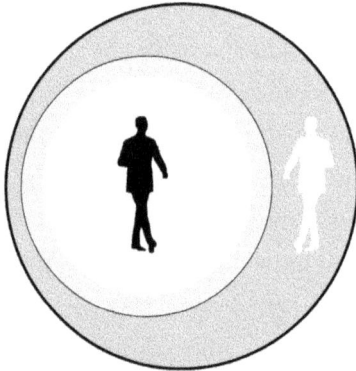

A negative image identity strengthens an endo-ideal's identity since it is just the same image in reverse. As the opposition, you need to define yourself as something other than the inverse of the endo-ideal.

Resistance needs a rallying vision for the future. You cannot ask people to jump into the unknown, or to support the negative image while they are still in a mental fog that rejects the negative image. That fog also causes people to seek out strong endogroups; they will find no security in a movement that seeks only to dismantle.

An effective resistance for those under dictatorship needs to present a vision of the future that is familiar, comforting, yet sparkling with hope and the removal of all that is bad in the present. The European Union has provided that vision for many European countries in their resistance against dictatorship. The state as a member of the EU is held up as nationalism but better, against the dictatorships that preach only nationalism. It is a weakened endogroup that is, at the same time, stronger due to alliances. You can design better methods of governance, including alternatives to statism and trading blocs, but present these as proposed evolution. Your starting place must be as the existing nation if you are to represent the existing nation.

In addition to identifying yourself, identify the dictator. Do not accept their self-identification as the leader of your country. Words like dictator, tyrant or oligarch still recognize a position of power which identifies them as the endo-ideal. These titles should be replaced with words like *usurper*, or any crime they have committed. Identify them as a criminal and a fraud. Syrians named Hafez Assad, *The Butcher of Damascus,* in recognition of his crimes, not his authority. People in the US refer to Trump as *the felon* instead of the president.

It is a very good idea to accuse the dictator of crimes. This casts them as the negative image of state authority. This is helpful in undermining the validity of their claim to represent that authority. Those who act as avid reflectors of state authority are likely to be made uncomfortable by these repeated reminders. If the dictator is acting in opposition to the recognized laws and principles of the endogroup, they must not be a genuine member of the endo-ideal. Use their crimes to convince their reflectors to uphold endogroup principles instead of the dictator. If you have successfully identified yourself as the rightful defender of the principles of the state or its people, you can convince reflectors to support your movement instead of the dictator.

In addition to upholding endogroup principles, convince regime reflectors that the dictator is acting in opposition to the endogroup itself and encourage them to defend the endogroup. The defeat of Viktor Orbán will depend on convincing Hungarians that Russia is the real threat to their identity and principles, not Ukraine, refugees, or the European Union. It is very important to counter attempts by the dictator to present themselves as the defender of the endogroup. Orbán's campaign against Ukraine isolates Hungary within the European Union, but he is hoping Hungarians can be convinced to fear Ukraine enough to isolate themselves under his rule. The worse life gets under dictatorships, the more susceptible people are to a tyrant presenting themselves as a strong defender.

Take control of the propaganda surrounding the dictator in the following ways:

> Do not grant them an identity as the legitimate ruler.

> Give them a negative image identity that assigns guilt.

> Identify yourselves as the true representatives of the state and its people.

> Depict them as the primary enemy of the people.

> Depict them and their reflectors as a separate endogroup destroying the state.

How To Dismantle a Dictatorship

Deny all claims to their superiority, great leaders, grand destiny, creation or persecution.

Focus on their crimes and illegitimacy.

Create and widely distribute your own history of the dictator and their endogroup.

Reject any attempt to conflate the regime with the will of the people.

Disrupt any event or institution where they appear in public as your representative, including your embassies.

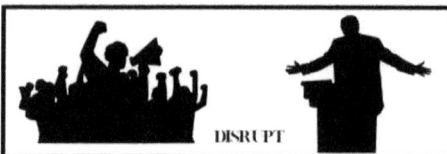

DELEGITIMIZE   IDENTIFY   ASSERT

CONDEMN   OTHER   DENY

EXPOSE   REFRAME   REJECT

DISRUPT

The endo-ideal relies on reflection from within the group, a negative image to transfer all guilt to, and recognition from other endo-ideals. Without these, the tyrant is no longer your dictator. Instead, they are just some guy that needs to be arrested.

Identify yourselves as the true representatives of the endogroup.

Identify the dictatorship as a fraud and an usurper.

The tyrant has no validity. In words and actions, never stop pointing that out.

How To Dismantle a Dictatorship

Step 2: Reject their reality

In an endogroup, individuals meld to create a shared will and a shared reality. Every committed person in the endogroup will follow and enforce the *laws of endoreality*. These laws are the most important thing to remember in this entire book. The tendency of a large part of society to uphold these laws is what upholds the dictatorship. When endoreality is not upheld, the structure of power collapses.

The laws of endoreality assign all ownership, virtue, credit and victimhood to the endo-ideal and all vice, debt, guilt and punishment to the negative image.

Insults generally reflect badly on those using them, not those assigned them. Using meaningless insults with the hope that others will shun the target seldom works beyond kindergarten, with one exception: this type of name-calling works very well for the endo-ideal. That is an effect of the laws of endoreality. The endo-ideal has the right to define. If they call someone a derogatory name, such as *bitch*, *loser*, or *thug*, the target will be cast as the negative image. If the same technique is attempted against an endo-ideal, it will not work, as long as the laws of endoreality are being enforced. It is more likely that insults will cause people to recognize the endo-ideal as a victim of hate because the laws of endoreality assign all victimhood to the endo-ideal.

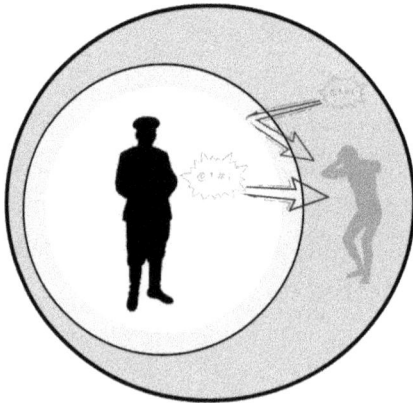

Tyrants use this power. This is how the US MAGA group were able to latch onto every perceived insult, from *deplorable* in 2016 to *garbage* in 2024, and use these insults as victimhood to strengthen their exceptional myth. Any valid criticism can be deflected in the same way. Pointing out Vladimir Putin's crimes was derided for years as being *Russophobic* and critics were accused of *McCarthyism*. Both of these words deflected Russian guilt and claimed victimhood in its stead. Even objecting to decades of atrocities by Benjamin Netanyahu or Paul Kagame will have critics attacked as *anti-semitic* or *pro-genocide*. If anyone else attempts to retaliate to the endo-ideal's name-calling, they will fail. That can only work when the laws of endoreality are widely being challenged and widespread contempt is being directed toward the dictator. In that case, it works because the tyrant is no longer recognized as an endo-ideal.

In an endogroup, reality is what the endo-ideal says and virtue is what they do.

How To Dismantle a Dictatorship

If you are opposing a dictatorship, it is much better to use verifiable facts because you do not have the ability to create endoreality. Only an endo-ideal can do that, and if you create another endo-ideal, your resistance will be a rival endogroup. Political opposition groups often fail to dismantle a dictatorship because they present as a rival endogroup, using the same baseless insults against their enemies and baseless claims of virtue for their endo-ideal. As a rival endogroup, they are seen as an existential threat, and they can end up strengthening the tyrant. If you want to weaken endoreality, instead of just replacing it, you have to use transparent, verifiable truth. That is how you lift people out of the emotional realm of endoreality and into conscious thought.

Endoreality is the powerful coercive force that holds the endogroup together. Endoreality is not judged as true or false, like facts in universal reality. It is centred on strength of belief instead of strength of evidence. It is a subjective, emotional reality that is only held within the endogroup. This is the type of belief that tells someone their partner would never hurt them when their partner is factually and evidently hurting them. This type of belief can also convince people that their dictator has a *master plan* where everything will turn out well, even when the dictator has openly stated plans for the opposite. Endoreality can allow people to deny genocide while participating in one and see prosperity and justice in poverty and crime.

Because this is an emotional response, outside of conscious effort or awareness, it is very difficult to counter. The intense level of belief in endoreality means it can become socially real within the endogroup. Race is not real, but racism can be real as lived social reality. Tyrants are not invincible or inevitable, but they can become very difficult to overcome in a society that views them as unassailable. This emotional truth that holds people under a dictatorship is the same as the bond that holds people in abusive relationships of all kinds.

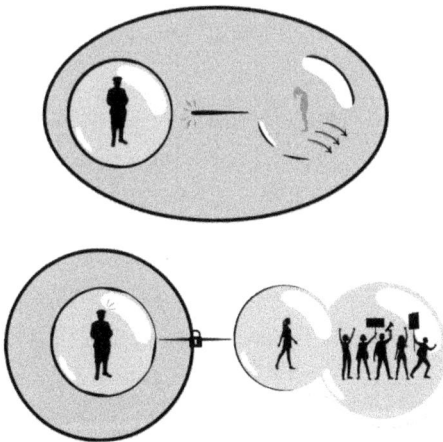

In this book, I will sometimes state reasons why endo-ideals, reflectors or the negative image behave in a certain way. This is not meant to imply that there is a master plan that anyone is following or that everyone is making conscious decisions about their behaviour. People committed to an endogroup are following the laws of endoreality, and their responses are ordered by their emotions. Emotional responses are near immediate. They require attentiveness and effort to overcome. Many people support, uphold and defend endoreality without recognizing what they are doing. Very few people in an endogroup have conscious awareness of what is happening or what role they are playing. Endoreality is a substitute for such awareness. Endoreality presents a version of events where all of the justifications are built in and all of the blame reassigned before any conscious awareness occurs.

Resisting endoreality requires continual, conscious awareness of everything around us. This is difficult for people that are confused, distracted and under stress, which is one reason people are kept in those states under totalitarian dictatorships. Even calm, healthy people are not designed for that level of intense focus on their daily lives. We all leave the vast majority of our responses and interpretations on auto-pilot and allow them to be handled by our emotional will. This frees our conscious will to analyze only the information that feels new or threatening. Endoreality is created through our common, everyday responses, by making the new look familiar and disguising the threatening as safe. Resisting tyranny must include sharing the task of necessary vigilance and helping others who may be unable to break free of endoreality on their own.

When attempting to challenge endoreality, think about the other principles the person probably holds which are in conflict with the dictatorship. To do this, try to find what other endogroup allegiances they hold and how strong those allegiances are. I once tried, for a very long time, to gain the support of a US-based influencer. I wanted him to oppose the US abduction and nearly 13-year-long torture and illegal confinement of a 14-year-old Canadian boy. This man was a committed male endo-idealist, so he had zero empathy for women and children. He was also committed to US, white and Christian endo-idealism, so I could not find empathy for a Canadian, Egyptian/Palestinian, Muslim boy. I finally had a breakthrough when I showed him that, under the Geneva Conventions, the boy was either a civilian or a prisoner of war. He did not care about the civilian part, but the fact that the US was torturing a prisoner of war shocked and horrified him. He was a committed supporter of my campaign from that point on, but it took me years to get to this one principle that resonated with him. Save yourself a lot of time and recognize the dominant endogroups of the person you are talking to before trying to appeal to them.

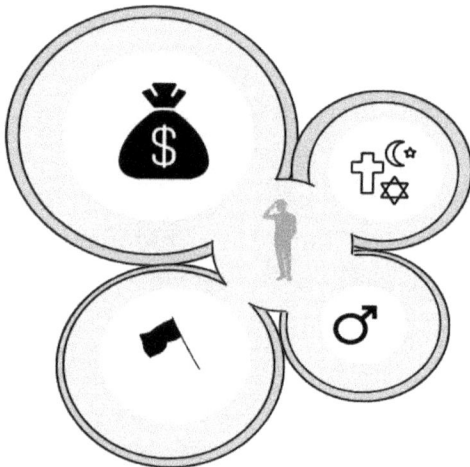

The former Chief Prosecutor at Guantanamo Bay, Colonel Morris Davis, is another man that did not seem to have any limits to what he would enthusiastically endorse if it came from the US military. He was in a court that was set up counter to all legal principles, to try the *victims*

of many international crimes. The court already used farcical evidence, witness tampering, and laws that were contradictory, created illegally, and applied retroactively. Davis acted as the outspoken attack dog for this entire black hole of legal justice until it finally triggered what must have been his sole remaining moral or legal principle. He eventually resigned in 2007 because he agreed that waterboarding was torture, and he was against evidence obtained under torture being admissible by the kangaroo court. If that truly was the reason he quit, he is one of many people that had a sudden revelation of morals triggered by something most would consider a minor aspect of a large injustice.

The endo-ideal dictator's power to create endoreality includes the ability to create subjective designations of criminality and insanity. In *The Creation of Me, Them and Us*, I explained that in an endogroup, *"The definition of insanity is disagreeing with endoreality and the definition of criminality is acting against the laws of endoreality."* A new dictatorship will invent new history, facts and laws and deny that old ones are real. They will designate opposition to them as insanity, treason, or heresy and employ authoritative figures such as psychologists, judges and priests to institute their decrees as authoritative fact.

Since all states are endogroups to some degree, many have created a world of authoritative endoreality that people are immersed in from birth. Challenging the legality of the Guantanamo trials would have you labelled as *anti-American*. Challenging psychologists means *you don't care about mental health*. Challenging academics makes you *anti-intellectual* or *pseudoscientific*. Arguments are not responded to with evidence, but with emotional name-calling. In such a world, no guiding principles are followed. It is all shifting, ephemeral endoreality, based on authoritative decrees.

In this world, it is very easy for a dictator to declare anyone criminal and insane. Those words have no universal meaning and vary by endogroup. It is also very easy to declare a president a king. Some authority can just write a paper outlining how a democratic system is closer to a monarchy than a democracy, and the name will be changed for *greater accuracy*. This is one example of how the creators of endoreality disguise the new as familiar, by claiming they *discovered* a thing they created. If you object, you will hear: *Omg, language evolves!*

You need to calm down! Why does it matter to you? It's basically the same thing! Why are you so obsessed? You just want to hate. And then they will assign a word to you, a word for a disbeliever or a heretic, and you too will be declared criminal and insane.

Charles Krauthammer was a psychologist who created a diagnosis of secondary mania as a variant of manic depression and helped create the third edition of the US psychologists' bible, the *Diagnostic and Statistical Manual of Mental Disorders* (DSM-III). He was also an influential columnist and political speechwriter who served on George W. Bush's Council on Bioethics. In 2003, this highly authoritative figure wrote a column in which he created a diagnosis of *Bush Derangement Syndrome* and *Murdoch Derangement Syndrome* to describe political opposition to those men. This diagnosis was picked up by some supporters of Barack Obama as *Obama Derangement Syndrome* and in the UK as *Thatcher Derangement Syndrome*, before it inevitably reappeared as *Trump Derangement Syndrome*. In February 2025, the *Psychology Today* blog suggested the diagnosis should be renamed *political anxiety disorder*.

In March 2025, a group of Minnesota state senators introduced a bill to classify Trump

Derangement Syndrome as a mental illness using Krauthammer's wording to describe it as a *"general hysteria"*. For those who watch psychology's role as a political bludgeon, yes, hysteria is the same word used to describe women as being insane because female. The diagnosis of hysteria was used to physically mutilate, torture and imprison women who offended men since the 5th century BCE. That is hardly the only example of psychology's role in upholding tyranny. The Guantanamo show trials used a quack psychologist for legitimacy, and so have many others. With all of the authoritative discussion surrounding Trump Derangement Syndrome, now with its very own acronym, TDS, nobody should be surprised when people start to be involuntarily confined for exhibiting signs of the latest version of this insanity diagnosis.

In parallel, current challenges to the US legal system are meant to ensure that an already highly subjective justice system, that was already a direct reflection of endoreality, becomes nothing more than the whim of a tyrant. The usurpation of justice systems and medical diagnosis by endoreality was a gradual development that took decades, or even centuries, to arrive at this point. The first step was in allowing word definitions and legal definitions to slip into subjective, fuzzy meaninglessness. When everything is uncertain and words are continually changing, people are deeply immersed in endoreality. The dictatorship is often the final step in a long process leading to this point.

If the laws of endoreality are the most important thing to remember in this entire book, countering them is the most important aspect of resistance. Usurp the right to define reality and refuse to reflect endoreality. This is the opposite of not believing in anything or being flexible with ephemeral, changing reality. Resistance requires an adherence to the provable facts in universal reality. It requires a rejection of relative judgement and words used as tools of endogroup shunning or inclusion. This cannot be accomplished by a rival endogroup that is immersed in its own endoreality.

Dictatorships have ministries of propaganda for a reason. Resisting a dictatorship requires organized effort in counter-propaganda, which analyzes and exposes subjective endoreality. It also requires the creation of reliable, universal knowledge that does not have subjective judgement baked in. So many years of coercive language can only be dismantled by focused effort. Change their words, change their language, but ensure that yours does not just recreate the problem as a negative image of the original.

Universal meaning is almost non-existent under longstanding dictatorships. It is required in order to avoid endoreality. Universal meaning has the following attributes:

> It does not require interpretation by academics, psychologists, judges, censors and other arbiters of authoritative reality.

> It does not vary based on subjective opinion.

> It is impartial about who it is applied to.

Weakening the endorealities of rival states with transparency and truth is a time-tested tactic used by enemy states. This is how the Kremlin got its foothold in the propaganda war against the west. Once people had their endorealities shattered, through the exposure of lies by their own governments, they were very susceptible to the bombardment of misinformation that followed. If easily accessible facts from transparent and reliable sources had been the norm, governments would not have been so vulnerable to this attack, and the current widespread refusal to trust authority would have been avoided. Learn from this mistake; fight propaganda with verified facts, not more propaganda.

The most powerful tool for shattering endoreality is humour.

There are several reasons so many dictatorships are wary of comedy. Laughter plays many roles in endogroups, as outlined in an entire chapter of *The Creation of Me, Them and Us*. Here are the ones most relevant to combatting endoreality:

Shared laughter is bonding.

Comedy can point out cognitive dissonance and shatter endoreality in a safe environment, using laughter to reduce the resulting anxiety and fear.

Comedy can effectively ridicule the
dictator.

Comedy can increase empathy for a
negative image.

From depictions of Xi Jinping as Winnie the
Pooh to stand up routines that ridicule
stereotypes, every level of comedy should be
used as much as possible to achieve these four
aims.

Fear is the primary catalyst for endogroup
formation, so the existential threat is a very
important piece of endoreality. Endogroups are
an emergency power structure created to
withstand existential threats. The group self is
formed in the minds of everyone so that all will
be willing to sacrifice for the group. The power
accumulated in the endo-ideal is meant to
enhance their ability to fight off the enemy.

Sometimes an existential threat exists.
Sometimes a revolution or war is fought against
a real existential threat and the revolutionaries
or fighters become tyrants, but it is rarely
necessary to keep a dictator to combat threats.
An endogroup was never meant to be a
permanent structure. It becomes a permanent
structure as a means to transfer guilt and retain
power. The original reason for its formation is
still key, however. Without the wide perception

of an external, existential threat, an endogroup will never be very strong. Therefore, the threat must be created, encouraged, and exaggerated in order to form and hold a strong endogroup.

Unnecessary obsession over external threats strengthens endogroups. Encourage people in this trap to develop other interests or just step away from the news and do something constructive. Endoreality is an emotional knowledge. It is strengthened when emotions are strong and weakened as the person feels calmer.

The following are ways to help combat endoreality:

Share the task of identifying endoreality.

Provide transparently verified truth as an alternative.

Highlight opposing principles to cause cognitive dissonance.

Use humour to create connection and empathy and to ridicule endoreality.

Reduce focus on existential threats to reduce endogroup strength.

Reject words or narratives which cast people as the endo-ideal or negative image.

Refuse to assign the group's vice and guilt to the negative image.

How To Dismantle a Dictatorship

Refuse to assign the group's virtue, credit or victimhood to the dictator.

A dictatorship will collapse when its endoreality is rejected. Use every opportunity to counter the laws of endoreality.

Step 3: Resist their will

A relationship is made up of constantly changing and diverse interactions. In *Abstracting Divinity*, I described three types of interaction: *connection, sublation* and *violation.* Connection results from balanced interactions, sublation occurs when interactions are dominated by one will, and violation is a forceful destruction of personal boundaries against a person's will.

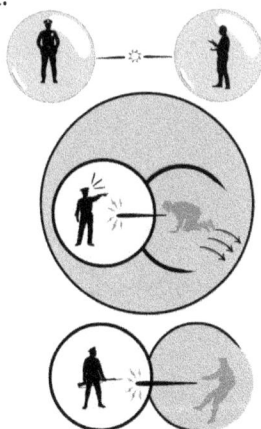

Security is derived from connection and power is derived from sublation and violation. This is why totalitarianism, like an abusive spouse, tries to eliminate all interactions that do not involve the state and increase the number of interactions dominated by the state. The more people that are sublated to the tyrant, and the more of their interactions the tyrant dominates, the more complete the tyrant's power. Your goal is to block both violation and connection, and reverse the flow of power in sublation, in every interaction with the dictatorship.

Do not obey anything you can possibly refuse. Recalcitrance can be used to drain the more powerful. Think of a toddler refusing to obey a parent, a student refusing to learn, or an employee refusing to work. Make it cost them more energy than they are demanding of you. Block interactions, stall interactions, make interactions as painful and frustrating as possible for the dictatorship. Resist everything, no matter how small. Bring everything to a standstill. Block movement, disobey, refuse orders, confuse bureaucrats, give false information, make mistakes, forget, tell lies, be late. Do whatever you can to consume as much of their time, energy and resources as possible in every interaction.

To treat the dictatorship as a separate endogroup, instead of an endo-ideal, you need to shun and disrupt connections with both the tyrants and their reflectors. They ought to be terrified to appear anywhere in public and distrustful of everyone around them. There is no security great enough to protect a tyrant who has lost the public's support. They ought to feel fear and doubt every day. They should never again be permitted to enjoy public interactions or freedom. Confront them with opposition everywhere they go, through graffiti, artwork, entertainment, protests and online. Force them to imprison themselves. Draw an endosocial barrier around the tyrant and those who support them.

No social interaction or exchange with the dictatorship should be willingly supported. Do not serve them. Do not host them. Do not permit their presence. If you cannot refuse service, forget to take their reservations, forget to give their food orders to the kitchen, take their deliveries to the wrong address, block their security, and put them in danger. If you cannot refuse information, make sure what you give them is wrong, and then deny you said it.

If you must work for their corporations, do everything possible to ensure that they lose more money and reputation than they gain from your labour. If a work shutdown is impossible, do a work slowdown. If disrupting your place of work is not helpful, disrupt public life. If it is not effective to work slowly, then drive slowly, walk slowly, shop slowly and conduct bureaucratic chores slowly. Use incompetence wherever possible. Lose the ability to read, remember, understand, hear or see when those abilities are needed for compliance. Know nothing about anything. Cry. Faint. Hyperventilate and have chest pains. Create time consuming disorder in all things. Break things, spill things, knock things over. Create disruption in everyday affairs wherever that is most inconvenient.

If you are forced to fight their wars, blow up their weapons depots. Tell their secrets, strengthen their enemies, alienate their allies, undermine their respect, reduce their capability and surrender to their enemy if at all possible. If their enemy is your ally, work with the enemy. This has been the path to liberation for many states, including the United States. The US is no longer a colony because France encouraged and supported the US resistance against England while France and England were at war.

In Thailand in 2014, anti-coup demonstrators were arrested for reading *1984* or using the three-finger salute from *The Hunger Games*. People then started announcing 'picnics' and eating sandwiches in public as a form of protest, and they were arrested for sandwich-eating. Dictatorships look increasingly ridiculous and weak as they criminalize increasingly unthreatening, everyday activities, and this makes them seem less formidable and more a target for humour.

Chinese resistance prefers ambiguous and deniable acts in order to circumvent the harsh crackdowns that meet any direct challenge. Similar to Thailand's vicious use of the lèse-majesté law to prevent any perceived criticism of the royal family, the Chinese Communist Party (CCP) prosecutes dissenters for acts *detrimental to the Chinese national spirit* or [which] *hurts the feelings of the Chinese people*. The CCP insists that *social harmony* requires unquestioning obedience to the dictatorship. Their inordinate fear of even *terroristic thoughts*, which are thoughts in opposition to the CCP, makes the public very wary of any open protest or resistance. Even discussing politics in private social settings has led to accusations of *inciting subversion of state power*.

For this reason, Chinese resistance in the early 2000s preferred a tactic called 'strolling'.

Instead of open meetings and large gatherings, people casually walk through the same area at the same time to create massive crowds. China usually responds to such provocations with its own indirect retaliation, such as 'street cleaning' with large vehicles spraying water in the area crowds are moving through. Still, these actions show both the CCP and the people the power of the over 1.4 billion people in China if they ever pitted themselves against the relatively tiny 1.5 million police. These acts of resistance have emboldened the public to conduct many huge regional protests over the years and often achieve political reforms.

Chinese resistance is an encyclopedia of indirect subversive tactics. The White Paper protests of 2022 used blank pieces of paper to symbolize censorship. The CCP responded by censoring blank paper and arresting people with blank paper with accusations that they were *picking quarrels and provoking trouble.* Due to early extreme censorship of online communication, Chinese resistance are masters of algorithm evasion and trend piggybacking. They have used the Friedmann equation to represent China opening up to freedom, homophones in place of words that would be censored, and images and videos to suggest a meaning as though they are playing a game of charades. During the 2011 protests called the Jasmine Revolution, the CCP eventually censored all plant names and many other words from social media in an attempt to stop the conversation. References to the Tiananmen Square protest have been referred to by a rolling series of implausible dates like January 36, or simply *that day*. People use repetition of positive and patriotic phrases to imply the opposite. They represent their own messages with out-of-context clips of speeches from political figures such as Xi Jinping. All of these tactics make the CCP and their censors the butt of a long-running, national joke.

In a strong enough totalitarian society, any act not instigated by the regime is resistance, especially if it has wide participation. In Chile, Pinochet's ten-year-old dictatorship made it very clear that he would respond to a proposed labour action on May 11, 1983, with a massacre by the military. The strike then became less overt and involved the entire population. Instead of openly striking, the first protest in many years was a national absenteeism and slowing – of everything. People worked slowly, drove slowly, swept the streets slowly, and moved in everything as if they were suddenly possessed by the spirits of sloths or tortoises. They ended the day by banging pots and continued on subsequent days with increasing subversion. People danced in the streets singing *Y va a caer! Y va a caer!* (And it will fall! And it will fall!) in the face of Pinochet's brutal repression of musicians. They held lightning strikes and protests that were over too quickly for the police to arrive. Participation in these actions emboldened the population until they could finally hold massive national strikes and, ultimately, achieve a fair election, in December, 1989.

An endogroup is a zero-sum game. Joy felt by one is seen as a robbery of others. Totalitarianism restricts joy in every way possible. Dismantling a dictatorship involves draining energy from the regime and pouring energy into its alternative. Effective resistance receives energy through laughing, talking, reading, sharing, and creating connections with others. When interacting with those outside the regime, add energy and create connections whenever possible. Sing, dance, wear colours, be creative, be generous and kind, share food, tell jokes, play tricks on the regime, make a game of resistance. Share grief and mourning so it is easier to bear. Reduce fear with laughter, connection, and loyalty to others. These are all methods to reduce sublation to the will of the tyrant.

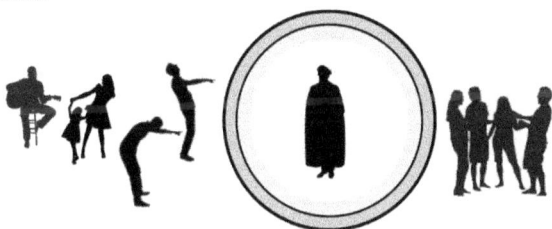

Sublation allows a tyrant to gain control over emotional responses and preempt conscious control over actions. Russia, China, and many other authoritarian states are held together purely by sublation. There is no way most dictatorships could survive without this emotional hold on the public. An effective resistance must trigger emotional responses to counter this attachment to the regime.

The collapse of the Berlin Wall is an example of the speed of collapse when sublation of a population is weakened. The 104-mile-long wall existed from 1961 until 1989. It separated families and loved ones and divided the city of

Berlin for 28 years. In 1989, the Iron Curtain was collapsing in an era of rare restraint from the USSR. Softening borders in Poland, Hungary and Czechoslovakia allowed East Germans a way to leave and gave them enough hope to begin having massive demonstrations. The Berlin Wall fell as part of a domino effect of endogroup softening. Watching others free themselves allows people to imagine themselves free. It expands their belief in what is possible.

Sometimes overthrowing a dictator is a result of a domino effect from a country's own history. Bolivia used to hold coups like people hold birthday parties. The country has had around 190 coups and revolutions in its 200 years of existence, and many more attempts, nearly all prior to 1984. Democracy in Bolivia is now enforced through publicly endorsed strikes, blockades, protests, and occasional marches on

La Paz. People are ready to react to political moves within hours or less.

In August 2016, I arrived in Potosi and experienced the instant political action Bolivians are known for. Potosi is a miners' town. The miners were having disagreements with the formerly allied federal government under Evo Morales over issues including environmental and human rights regulations. This was not one of the many peaceful strikes for reasonable causes that are ongoing somewhere in Bolivia nearly every day. In this case, multinational corporations were using the strength of autonomous miners' resistance as a proxy to bypass environmental and safety regulations. The Deputy Interior Minister sent to negotiate was kidnapped and horribly murdered, resulting in more violence on both sides.

It was eye-opening how little discussion took place before the town mobilized. When I checked in at the place I was staying, I was told to go get a lot of groceries immediately because I would be there for days or weeks and everything would be shut. In 2010, a *bloqueo* in Potosi had lasted three weeks, so I started looking for a way out instead. I was told no one was going to take the risk of assisting, but someone did, and drove me to a spot where I could see the bus station. There were two children, around eight years old, blocking the road to the station with a piece of string they held up across it. The taxi driver immediately stopped when the children issued him a challenging stare. I exited the car with my bags and walked like an oblivious foreigner to the bus station the children were blockading. I got to the station with no rocks thrown at me and bought a seat on an empty bus for the regular fare.

The bus driver pulled out with only a couple of us on board, but he did not take the road that would have had us out of town in 10 minutes. Instead he spent an extra half an hour circling the outskirts of town on roads not built for buses until we arrived at the main road outside Potosi, beyond the already barricaded exit point. Relief lasted for a few kilometres until we ran into the next blockade, where dozens of buses and other vehicles were already stopped. The drivers eventually negotiated passage with the blockaders for the two emptiest buses and began selling exorbitantly priced tickets on those buses to meet whatever passage fee was negotiated. My guardian angel was working overtime because I was on one of those two buses and I was left 'asleep' instead of charged extra.

This was very fortunate because I had no money left, one of the reasons I couldn't go buy enough food to sit out a blockade. At that point, I had two bank cards, one from a bank in Montenegro and one from a bank in Argentina. Both banks had decided that anyone in Bolivia must be up to no good and blocked my cards. So when I eventually arrived in Sucre, I had no place booked and no money to go find one. As I was looking around to see where the safest place to sleep that night would be, a man came over from the bus depot tourism booth and asked if I needed a place to stay. I explained that I was just looking for a safeish place to crash outside or in the station because my bank cards weren't working, and he said, *don't worry about it, you can pay me whenever.* I took the trust fall and ended up staying a month in his beautiful rental overlooking the plaza, despite it taking the first week to convince the bank in Montenegro (but not the one in Argentina) that my card had gone to Bolivia on purpose and not for nefarious activity.

There are several countries and many regions with strong anarchist networks that step up when government fails or acts against the people. Some regions exist in a continual state of suversion of authority. I don't personally know any that can rival the ability to handle any situation that comes up with the speed and confidence of most Bolivians. There is no hesitation, no waiting to see how things turn out, or for someone in authority or others to do something. Willingness to subvert or ignore official processes and find immediate solutions as problems arise is a product of strong networked resistance to two centuries of instability. No matter what kind of forces are behind political turmoil, everyone in Bolivia knows the drill. No one wonders how it will turn out because everyone knows exactly what could happen and how important it is that they react with speed and intelligence at each step. Countries that idly watch dictatorships and coups assemble over weeks, months, years and even decades, could learn a lot from Bolivia. So could democracies that patiently wait for elections as their government gets worse under each administration.

Countries where the people respond instantly to political moves are the true democracies. South Korea showed the world what that looked like in 2024 when the sitting president, Yoon Suk Yeol, attempted to declare martial law. Thousands of protesters hit the streets immediately, forcing the order to be lifted six hours after it was declared. The president was then forced to step down and tried for impeachment. Like Bolivia, South Korea has muscle memory of dictatorships, martial law and their last coup, in 1979.

Since independence in 1960, Burkina Faso has had coups in 1966, 1980, 1982, 1983, 1987, 2014, January 2022, and September 2022. Every change in head of state has been the result of a coup. In 2014, the president was Blaise Compaoré. Compaoré had conducted both the 1983 coup to place Thomas Sankara in power and the 1987 coup where he had his friend Sankara and 12 government officials assassinated to place himself in power. In 2014, he was about to change the constitution to extend his 27 year rule. The long-suffering Burkinabè began to march on October 28th, with women waving wooden spoons in protest. Protesters faced down bullets with rocks, set fire to parliament on the 30th, and by the 31st, with several people dead, Compaoré announced his retirement from his new home in Côte d'Ivoire.

On the 31st, I counted five government and military officials who announced themselves as the new leader. Compaoré himself announced a transition period of a year or 90 days during which he would continue as the leader.

Protesters had to continue until they finally achieved a democratic election in the fall of 2015, a year after they toppled the dictatorship. After all that, extremist violence unleashed on the country resulted in a military coup in January, 2022. Nine months later, Ibrahim Traoré conducted another coup to install himself as a more Russia-friendly military dictatorship.

Such a history would seem sufficient to discourage any population. Certainly, it would discourage those who refuse to protest a coup against their democracy because *I protested years ago and it didn't make a difference.* Democracy is not a sport for quitters or those who wait and see. Democracy will ultimately be for those who persist, like Bolivia and Burkina Faso, and those who rise immediately at the first sign of dictatorship, like South Korea. Democracy is not a vote every few years. Democracy is the expression of will in every interaction. Freedom is the daily refusal to accept sublation. Governance by the people requires the people to act.

Heather Marsh

Power is the result of energy gained in interactions. To stop the flow of power, sublation and violation must be resisted and reversed in every interaction. Hold to your dignity, your autonomy, and your own will in every interaction with a dictatorship.

How To Dismantle a Dictatorship

Step 4: Block validation

Endo-ideals, reflectors, and the negative image are roles played by people in an endogroup. When I use those terms, I am referring to anyone who is adopting these endogroup roles, whether they remain in the role for a minute or a lifetime. The characteristics described do not have to be permanent, and people do not adopt the same role in all situations. Even an endo-ideal can voluntarily drop their role. The goal of anyone trying to dismantle a power structure is to recognize who is adopting these roles and encourage them to gain awareness and change their behaviour. A deeper understanding of the emotional and cognitive impact of abandoning these roles is developed in *How to Survive the*

End of Empires. In this book, we focus on recognizing and countering the roles.

All endogroup roles adopt the perspective of the endo-ideal and uphold the laws of endoreality. The reflectors act as the endogroup police, reprimanding, tattling, and shunning anyone seen as insufficiently obsequious to the endo-ideal. Reflectors will manufacture justifications and denials, seize credit, and donate all their free time and money to uplift their endo-ideal. They will sabotage and attack the negative image or other reflectors if any try to rise. Reflectors are the primary creators and enforcers of endoreality.

The rise of techno-fascism is an example of endo-ideal creation by reflectors. Reflectors in the media and general public supported, promoted, and defended technology that has advanced a steady progress of tyranny for decades. They worshiped incompetent men in software development and cheered as they watched them collapse distributed industries into global empires of billionaires, surveillance and control.

Before the 1980s, IBM promoted computer programming as a *good job for girls*. It was a job that required meticulous attention to detail and involved long, tedious, and difficult hours of work, with no recognition and little reward. By the 1990s, the job had become incredibly easy, relative to what it had been before. The foundations had been painstakingly built through the work of women like Ada Lovelace, who created the first computer algorithm, Hedy Lamarr, who created the technology behind wireless communications, and Admiral Grace Hopper and other women who created the first compilers and high level programming languages. The tedium and slowness of writing in assembly code and performing frequent mechanical repairs on a giant computer were removed for later software developers. It was time for the demographic that created hostile corporate takeovers in the 1970s and stock market manipulation in the 1980s to jump in on their new get-rich-quick scheme.

These men, and their uncritical fans, created the dot-com bubble of the 1990s and subsequent crypto and tech startup booms and busts. Venture capital flooded into the pockets of an army of men in their teens and 20s with little education, no experience, and few business plans, as women in tech were elbowed out. First came Bill Gates, who had risen to notoriety in 1975 with his *An Open Letter to Hobbyists,* railing against the *"stealing"* and *"theft"* of software. In

1995, he and a complicit media convinced the world that the internet came in a box containing Windows 95 software. With a public who had no understanding of what the internet was, and no blogs or social media to fact check his media reflectors, they created a viral frenzy around a misinterpreted product. Win95 was not misunderstood simply because of misinformation; the public didn't want to understand it. They just wanted to buy the thing, support the genius, and believe all their problems would be solved. Gates became the richest man in the world, and the floodgates were opened.

From that point forward, unqualified men were told they had a *hacker mentality* despite a complete lack of skills, and highly skilled women were depicted as *your mom*, an idiot that cannot understand technology. Any man even marginally involved in technology was referred to as a *genius*, a *guru*, and someone whose vision was going to save the world. *I, for one, welcome our new hacker overlords*, said the repurposed meme.

The creation of an endogroup begins with the persecution and shunning of the lowest negative image before it scales up to the world. The lowest negative image in society is a woman, children, or both, for reasons explored in the *Binding Chaos* series. The root of tech-fascism, like all totalitarianism, was the early misogyny, or male endo-idealism. The women that remained in tech were sometimes allowed to work, but they were not allowed to succeed. Startup funding has poured into tech projects since the 2000s, but the amount that went to women remained very close to 0% for many years. When a woman did receive funding, it was usually a small amount to do something related to women, not industry dominance or world governance, and she usually needed men to be listed as co-founders. Credit, speaking positions, and media coverage of women also remained very close to 0%.

As a software developer, I experienced all of this firsthand. There were over one hundred people in my graduating class. Less than ten were women. I was the only one in my cohort of twenty. People would expect me to join them in marvelling over how brilliant my classmates or co-workers were, when I was doing the same job, often much better. People would offer jobs and funding to any man standing next to me, for ideas that were mine. Any achievement of mine was attributed to my anatomy. *Heather's boobs got an A! Heather's boobs got a job!*

In reality, I was rejected for jobs because managers told me I *didn't look like a software developer* or I *didn't match the culture*. At my first job as a software developer, my manager asked if I had gone over my ideas with my boyfriend, who he didn't know anything about. I was left outside of business social events to talk to the administration staff and girlfriends, the only other women. If I was a listed keynote speaker at a conference, or attending meetings, I would ask for my name tag and it would be handed to the man next to me. If the man said, *No, her*, they would give us both one because I must be the assistant. If I was speaking, people would ask if I was presenting *the user perspective* or sent in place of the busy man who must have come up with my ideas. Media constantly ask me *how I met Anonymous* or asked if I *could put them in touch with someone* from Anonymous, Wikileaks or other tech-adjacent movements that I was obviously a core part of. The endoreality was very clear: men were tech gods, and women were your stupid mom.

This was not just a casual expectation that only men would be software developers. Reflectors were policing this as an endoreality. There was extreme hostility and scepticism towards women succeeding in these fields.

Occasionally, that hostility came from men I worked with but, much more often, it came from the adoring reflectors. They had an image of the tech gods that were going to save them all, and I wasn't it.

At the same time, reflectors were willing to believe anything from unqualified men, or even invent achievements. I have repeatedly seen startup funders gush over men who were showing them existing commercial apps that they presented as their own. Worse, I once sat in an audience where a group of men described an app they wanted to develop that turned lights on and off. They demonstrated by having an assistant clearly flick a light switch on and off. The audience of funders later insisted that the lights were turned off by the app, which was not developed yet. These audiences were seeing miracles as clearly as any cult.

Men from every demographic succeeded in technology development, but they only reached the top if they followed a certain ideology: the ideology of power. Infatuated blindness encouraged the general public to give these men the authority to govern the world. Developing the algorithms that the world runs on is world governance, yet there was no restraint on what these algorithms were and are allowed to do.

Those in power maintained that governance was accomplished by a vote every several years, and the majority of the public chose to believe it. Believing that a vote every several years is self-governance and ignoring the algorithms creating the mazes everyone is required to run in is acceptance of endoreality over fact. It is an abdication of will and control over your own destiny. It is acceptance of the role of a reflector in a dictatorship.

A long time ago I mentioned that there was going to need to be some sort of international awareness and consensus over the increasing use of the electromagnetic field, which is a global commons. No one else agreed that consultation was necessary, and it wasn't. Neither was it necessary when data centres were placed in the ocean to contribute to ocean noise pollution and temperature change. When I said proof-of-work blockchain was an environmental disaster that I would never support, I was shouted down as a Luddite. Couldn't I see that cryptocurrency was going to overthrow the evil banks? And the new tech revolutionaries would be so much better? Now outer space is their personal garbage dump. The unregulated invasion of the global commons has met with nearly no resistance or oversight, worldwide. This is not solely the developers' fault. Reflectors bear some responsibility for the tyrants they created.

This unbridled power did not accumulate because no one knew it would happen. I am friends with many other developers who also worked to stop it and warn people. I also have many mutual acquaintances with some of the key players that created this, including one currently hailed as a *philosophy guru* working to collapse the United States and convert it to a feudal monarchy. People would gather at technology and social events and discuss the change we were all participating in. *Oh, there will be blood!* some would say cheerfully, as though concern over something so trivial made me less of a visionary than them. But when I proposed developing technology to bring in a true golden era, I, and others like me, were dismissed as naive and utopian. If it didn't involve creating unlimited power, it would go against human nature, at least the version of human nature experienced by these people.

But we both existed. Unlike Us was started at the end of 2011 as *"a research network of artists, designers, scholars, activists and programmers who work on 'alternatives in social media' ... to both analyze the economic and cultural aspects of dominant social media platforms and to propagate the further development and proliferation of alternative, decentralized social media software*". Many of my friends in that and other groups, loosely gathered around universities, hacklabs, and pro-democracy initiatives, were very aware of the dangers of tech-fascism and were working on alternatives. People trying to build prosocial architecture and help humanity were right there, right beside the techno-fascist-monarchist hyphenated ideologues who were plotting to destroy it. No amount of horrible politics, antisocial behaviour, general stupidity, and incompetence could deter the laws of endoreality that insisted on placing the predators at the top.

Reflectors chose power, because they always do. Reflectors are part of an endogroup structure, and endogroups are a structure for creating emergency power. A reflector will always support the powerful and create tyranny. It's their whole job.

The men these reflectors made into oligarchs are a large part of the tyranny we all now have to dismantle. They are very, very rich and in positions of great power all over the world because reflectors insisted they looked like geniuses who were going to save the world. They didn't say they were. Their reflectors did. They have been openly writing and speaking about what they were going to do for decades. There has been evidence of it for decades. They were chosen by the reflectors because of what they are.

The primary conflict in a dictatorship is not between the tyrant and the people. If it was, no dictatorship would last more than a day. Almost all conflict is between the reflectors and the negative image. From The Creation of Me, Them and Us: "Commonly called 'competition', the reflector-negative image struggle is the primary struggle within an endogroup. It pits the obedient reflectors against the ostracized negative image in a zero-sum struggle for the approval of the endo-ideal. It occupies all force that may otherwise be directed against the endo-ideal."

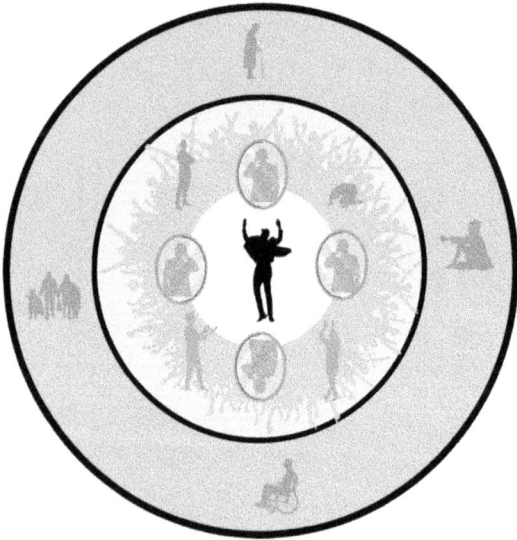

Tyranny is not created by tyrants. It is created by reflectors. Almost all endogroup conflict is reflectors fighting with anyone who tries to resist oppression or stop the creation of tyranny. Reflectors will insist that their tyrant is different, this one is going to save the world, this one has victimhood, superiority and a great destiny. They will deny the words the tyrant speaks and insist he meant something else. They will deny his deeds and deflect guilt onto his victims. They will react with extreme hostility, vindictiveness and violence to anyone who blocks the tyrant's path to power.

Reflectors uphold tyranny in another key way as well. When opposition to the tyrant forms, reflectors will attack those who want real change and uphold opportunists. Even when they oppose one tyrant, they will attempt to promote a new tyrant in their place. From political opposition leaders to NGOs to revolutionary leaders, they will attach themselves to a new strongman and defend the rise of a new tyranny.

People adopting the role of reflectors need to be educated. Their loyalty must be challenged and their allegiance broken. In the long run, the world needs to stop creating the conditions which motivate people to act as reflectors. A reflector is seen as obedient and selfless and so avoids the guilt and shame assigned to the negative image. When people do not feel overwhelming guilt and existential threat, they will not seek out and create permanent power structures.

People act as reflectors when they lack a strong will of their own. This may be because they have been denied the opportunity to form a strong will through conscious effort and sustained focus throughout childhood and beyond. It may also be because they have abdicated their own will. The most common reasons for someone to relinquish their own will are fear and shame, which is why those are the primary tools used to create endogroups. Endogroups require external enemies because the threat creates fear. Endogroups oppress others because guilt creates shame. Fear and shame cause people to adopt the role of reflectors, and the reflectors create endogroups.

ENDO-IDEAL ATROCITIES

THE NEGATIVE IMAGE

ANYONE OUTSIDE THE ENDOGROUP

If you want to dismantle a dictatorship, reflectors are going to be your primary obstacle. Even if they appear to have joined forces with you, they will continually sabotage the effectiveness of your efforts. This is not because they are horrible people, although they may be. Their defence of the endogroup and endo-ideals is an emotional response to fear and guilt. It is not something they are consciously aware of, any more than they are aware of their fear and guilt.

These are all ideas that are developed extensively in the *Binding Chaos* books. What you need to be aware of here is this:

> Your primary opposition is going to come from reflectors.

> Reflectors are motivated by fear and shame.

> Reflectors are acting on emotional reactions that they are not consciously aware of.

> Reflectors need safety and a way to acknowledge and address their shared endogroup guilt.

Once a reflector can be made to understand and recognize their emotional responses, they can be very valuable in resistance. Their nature to be complicit to power means they will attach to any power, especially if they have lost their previous endo-ideal. They will have a strong drive to redeem their newly accepted guilt which can make them very altruistic and motivated to work. They are susceptible to joining a revolutionary endogroup to atone for their complicity in the tyranny, but they can be recruited to an altruistic path instead.

Reflectors can be converted with words. It just takes an exhausting amount of effort. It is absolutely necessary, however. No tyranny will ever fall while reflectors are still creating and promoting tyrants. You can save time in trying to convert a dedicated reflector by learning what they don't care about:

> Endo-ideal atrocities: They have already reconciled this using the laws of endoreality. They will blame the victim. They may acknowledge the atrocities but say the tyrant must be upheld to avoid the greater evil. They may refuse to listen and say it doesn't affect them, or it is too stressful.

> The negative image: Everything in an endogroup is a zero sum game. If the negative image rises, the reflectors will become the negative image. They know this, and they will fight to prevent it from happening.

> Anyone outside the endogroup: Their entire focus is on their own endo-ideal. Boredom is an avoidance response that keeps them from engaging with any other topics.

So how can you convert them?

Find their dominant endogroups. The dominant endogroup is the one they feel most bonded to. If you ask yourself questions like who you would die for, or give your last cookie to, you can measure which of your endogroups are the most dominant. Appeal to them emotionally by referencing this endogroup. Many people are endoselves, who would only die for or give their last cookie to themselves. In this case, trigger emotions related to their own self-preservation.

Find their authoritative endogroups. Many people have told me that they are independent thinkers, completely free of outside influence, but nobody is. Humans are not designed with the ability to consciously make every decision themselves; everyone has trusted sources of authority. Find theirs. Even the most ardent reflector of a tyrant sometimes has other sources, laws, institutions, or people that they respect. If you can find one of these, you can appeal to them consciously by getting them to look at facts which contradict their endoreality. This is the most popular approach taken online, but its effects are usually transient. Endoreality will usually take over again because their emotional will is stronger and more immediate than their conscious will. If you have a success with this method, be sure to follow it quickly with emotional messaging to remove their attachment from the endo-ideal.

Use anger and fear to reverse their energy flow to the endo-ideal. Calm their fears and attempt to direct their anger towards the endo-ideal.

Use contempt and shame to reverse the flow of guilt from the endo-ideal. If you can find a way to trigger contempt for the endo-ideal, the reflector will see them as the negative image. If you can help them to process guilt and replace shame with dignity you can weaken their attachment to the endo-ideal.

Give them a new endo-ideal. This is what political parties try to do. It is expedient, but should be avoided if possible. Abstract ideas such as religions, patriotism, or male endo-idealism can be just as dangerous as a tyrant. Tread carefully.

In a dictatorship, a special class of reflectors are corporations and foreign governments that uphold the economy and government functioning. Corporations and foreign politicians may occasionally respond to education. They will always respond to economic ruin.

Go for the most powerful reflectors and the reflectors that are easiest to convert first. Reflectors have little practice exercising their own will. They are followers who are accustomed to frequent changes in endoreality. Most have little ego barring them from changing allegiance. When the tide turns against their endo-ideal, all but the most fanatical will follow the tide. For this reason, it is very important that they see other reflectors turning.

IDENTIFY DOMINANT ENDOGROUP

IDENTIFY AUTHORITATIVE ENDOGROUPS

REDIRECT FEAR AND ANGER

TRIGGER CONTEMPT AND ASSIGN GUILT

AVOID OFFERING A NEW ENDO-IDEAL

PRESSURE INSTITUTIONS

FOCUS ON KEY REFLECTORS FIRST

No tyrant can hold power without reflectors. The tyrant is a creation of reflectors.

How To Dismantle a Dictatorship

Step 5: Assign guilt

On February 28, 2025, Ukrainian President Volodymyr Zelensky traveled to the United States for a diplomatic meeting. While there, in front of journalists and the world, he was both attacked and humiliated by the Trump regime. Trump screamed until his face was red and physically invaded Zelensky's personal space. None of the crowd assembled against this one man let him speak. They shouted in the face of his calmness. They lied about his and Ukraine's actions and tried to force him to accept Russian propaganda as truth. They ordered him to appease the Russian aggressors invading his country and committing atrocities against Ukrainians in their home. They accused him of ingratitude and disrespect. One even insulted the clothes he wore. When they were finished, reflectors in the US media piled on and continued the same messaging.

As we discussed in the last chapter, the two most powerful emotional tools used to sublate one person to another are fear and shame. Anger and contempt are used to trigger those emotions. I refer to these processes in the *Binding Chaos* series as the *anger-fear symbiosis* and the *contempt-shame symbiosis*. Anger and fear are used to effect a transfer of energy, resulting in power for the angry person. Contempt and shame are used to effect a transfer of guilt, resulting in shame and humiliation for the victim. Both of these are used to create an endo-ideal of the person using anger and contempt and a negative image of the person reacting with fear and shame. These types of interactions must be resisted at all costs.

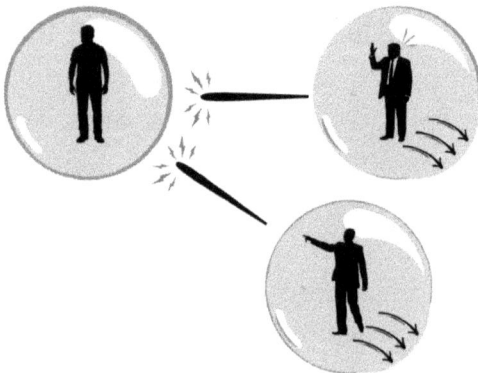

The extreme bullying by the pro-Kremlin US regime was an attempt to use anger and contempt to instill fear and shame in the Ukrainian President, the representative of the Ukrainian people. That meeting was filled with examples of attempted sublation. Guilt assignment, energy depletion and predation were all deployed. The attacks on Zelensky's person, through physical encroachment and insults on his character and clothing, were an attempt to destroy his inner circles of self. These are the methods dictators use to seize and hold power through sublation. In this case, it did not work.

Zelensky, in that meeting, was a model of how such interactions should be dealt with. He resisted all attempts to force him to respond in a way that could be used against him. He did not react to the aggression with fear or the attempts to humiliate him with shame. He left with his dignity intact. The people who lost all dignity in that interaction were the aggressors, who had their aggressive energy turned against them.

This meeting illustrated what happens when you refuse to accept the endoreality dictated by the endo-ideal and you resist the tyrant's will, as recommended in *Step 3*. One man used all the energy in that room, occupied an entire media cycle, and refused to be sublated. That is how you use up all the resources of the dictatorship. They cannot afford to expend this much energy. We are many; they are few.

Dignity has a special meaning in the *Binding Chaos* series of books. The definition is ownership over the innermost interactions which make up a self. This ownership creates personal integrity and strength. It requires freedom of thought, communication, association, interaction, and movement, physical autonomy, reputation and personal privacy. Free will and a network of balanced connections support personal dignity. It was obvious in that meeting that would-be tyrants see such dignity as an obstacle to their power. It is. That is why dictatorships attempt to strip dignity from those held under them.

Immediately after this meeting, Russia greatly increased the murder of Ukrainian civilians and destruction of Ukrainian civil infrastructure. The meeting included a pre-emptive attempt at guilt reversal. The wildly inaccurate accusations directed against Zelensky, that he was ungrateful and disrespectful and that he could stop Russia's invasion at any time, were used to blame him for the war crimes of Russia and the complicity of the US against him. The accusations of his supposed 'debt', which does not exist, were an attempt to justify violence against Ukraine.

Once guilt has been revealed, it will be assigned. If it does not attach to the accused, it will attach to the accuser. Because the Trump regime's attempt to reassign guilt failed, they were left shamed in front of the world. Guilt and shame are the province of the negative image, not an endo-ideal. This catalyst and similar events have caused the global image of the US as an endo-ideal to slip. The global public is increasingly returning anger and contempt back to the Trump regime. Anger creates the separation needed to block interactions of sublation. Contempt removes the dictatorship from the endo-ideal position and shuns them. These results have both been widely in evidence in the international response to the Trump regime.

Guilt assignment has been the preferred method used by the powerful to remove ethical people from government recently. This has been seen in many corporate coups in South America, including Paraguay (2012), Brazil (2016), and Bolivia (2019). Decades ago, popular leaders were assassinated, and many of those leaders are still inspiring others. Now they are much more effectively accused and tried in court, usually for whatever their opposition is most guilty of. Guilt is far more likely to stick if it is transferred instead of invented.

An assignment of guilt can be used to cast an endo-ideal as a negative image. It is an effective and thorough way to rid yourself of a dictator.

Guilt is important in Binding Chaos theory as a key element underlying the formation of societies. It is the foundation of law, economics, and even government, and it has a great influence on daily social interactions and emotions. The following are important points to remember about guilt and how it circulates:

In an endogroup, guilt is shared.

Within an endogroup, guilt and innocence are attached to roles instead of actions. The endogroup transfers its guilt to the negative image.

Accusing someone of wrongdoing will cast them as the negative image.

Guilt can only be felt through empathy. Hatred and anger act as barriers to empathy, so hatred and anger are encouraged in endogroups.

The desire to avoid guilt keeps the endo-ideal and reflectors strongly bonded to the endogroup.

Shame and fear keep the negative image strongly bonded to the endogroup.

Those outside will attribute collective guilt to everyone in the endogroup and shun them.

Shame and hatred will cause those in the endogroup to isolate themselves from those outside.

Shared isolation will increase bonding to the endogroup.

People burdened by guilt and shame will exhibit many symptoms of social paralysis.

How To Dismantle a Dictatorship

As cruelty increases and guilt accumulates, resistance appears to be more impossible.

Abuse becomes a cycle because there is always fresh guilt to be redeemed which leads to more people being punished and more horrific punishments.

SHARED GUILT

ATTACHED GUILT

ASSIGNED GUILT

EMPATHY

HATE & SHAME

ABUSE CYCLE

Assignment of guilt to a negative image is a key component holding the endogroup together. Reversing this is essential to dismantle the power structure. This is why many revolutions or liberation movements are preceded by some form of consciousness raising in which guilt is rejected by the negative image and assigned to the oppressor. If that reassignment can be made to stick, those in the endo-ideal may be cast as the negative image.

Making guilt stick to the endo-ideal is difficult. The steps an endogroup will take in response to accusation against an endo-ideal were outlined in *The Creation of Me, Them and Us*. These steps, detailed below, are all attempts to transfer or reduce guilt.

> Accuse the accuser. Probably the most common counter accusations use the *secret chamber* or *forbidden chamber* guilt that is described in *The Creation of Me, Them and Us*. These counters take the focus off of an endo-ideal's crimes and put it onto the discovery of the crimes. Official secrets and national security laws primarily exist to create such forbidden chambers so that people can be prosecuted for the discovery of an endo-ideal's guilt. This is *Why were you looking at my phone?* scaled up to the level of world leaders. Other accusations include *Why now?* which claims that the accusation may be valid, but the accusers' timing will aid enemies, or the endo-ideal is under too much stress, or it was *in the past,* and they have changed. Finally, people may

agree that the accusation was valid, but claim there was something wrong with *the way it was handled*. They insist they would have supported the victim if only she had smiled more or he had worn a suit or they had *followed proper procedure*.

Vilify the accuser as the negative image who can't be trusted to tell the truth. The endo-ideal is referred to as the businessman, billionaire, king, president, philanthropist, police or other endo-ideal title. The accuser is referred to as a terrorist, prisoner, prostitute, drug addict, or any other negative image designations based on sex, class, ethnicity, age and more.

Centre the perpetrator, transfer agency to the victim, and depict the perpetrator as passive, helpless, coerced or victimized. This is what is happening when a headline that should say: *Man shot by police* is written as: *Police facing inquiry over officer-involved shooting* or a statement that should be: *He broke her jaw* is stated as: *She's broken her jaw*.

Assert that due to the exceptional superiority of the endo-ideal, all of their actions are justified and too subtle for common understanding. This is where official titles and words like *the economy*, *the law* and *national security* are invoked to demand different rules for actions that would otherwise by recognized as criminal. The accuser's credentials are ridiculed and their comments are dismissed as *unqualified* and *uninformed.*

Assert that due to the exceptional victimhood of the endo-ideal, all of their actions are justified as their *right to exist* and any criticism is a *wish to kill them.* Exaggeration is used to increase the perceived harm facing the endo-ideal, in order to depict aggression as *self-defence.*

Downplay the effect of the actions on the victim. The victim will be told they *liked it* or *wanted it* or *if they didn't want it to happen why did/didn't they* ___. In a tyranny, this includes pointing out any benefits people received from the state, telling them they could have removed the tyrant if they wanted to, and to move if they don't like it. The accuser will be accused of benefiting in some way by gaining money, political power, fame or position. This is an attempt to convince the public that the victim is already receiving reparations and is not owed any more. The victim may even be accused of coming out ahead due to the crimes committed against them.

Exaggerate the effect of the accusation on the endo-ideal. This is seen in common headlines placing the predator as the subject and asserting that they are *under attack, facing down claims, hit by accusations, pressured, hounded, facing an onslaught of criticism, pursued by the law,* and *haunted by their past.*

Assert that the action was a sacrifice the endo-ideal made to benefit others. They are acting in *service to the country* to *keep you safe, restore the economy, give people jobs, remove harmful people from society,* create a great future or return to a great past. The claim that atrocities are committed in service to society is a transference of guilt to society. The claim of service is to establish that society owes them a debt.

If you successfully counter all of these defences, a tyrant can be assigned guilt. However, if that guilt is not also redeemed, it can be used to recreate the dictatorship. Unredeemed guilt is one of the two causes of endogroups that we talked about in the beginning of the chapter. How to ensure guilt is redeemed is a topic that will be explored in greater detail in *How to Survive the End of Empires.* For the purpose of this book, we just need to highlight one important aspect for resistance, which is to avoid incurring unnecessary guilt of your own.

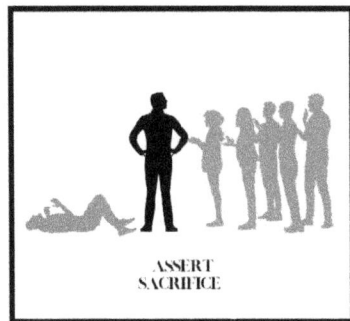

ACCUSE THE ACCUSER

VILIFY

CENTRE THE PERPETRATOR

ASSERT EXCEPTIONAL SUPERIORITY

ASSERT EXCEPTIONAL VICTIMHOOD

DOWN PLAY

EXAGGERATE

ASSERT SACRIFICE

Usually, the reason to not use violence as a first choice against a dictator is obvious. The dictator controls the military, police and prisons. The people have numbers. If you are choosing battles, choose the ones that play to your strengths, not your enemy's. Use methods that can involve everyone in society, including elders, children, and people with disabilities. In most cases, the majority of a population will not choose violence first, so you are limiting your resistance movement if that is what you choose. Violence may also cause any retaliation to be justified in the eyes of many who may otherwise have joined the resistance. Violence will be seen as a threat, and threats are the most potent building material for creating hardened endogroups.

Defensive violence often becomes unavoidable, but strategic violence, more commonly known as terrorism, has also been the tool of choice for many fighting against tyrants. *Propaganda of the deed* is an idea advocated by Italian anarchist Carlo Pisacane in 1857, which later appeared in Mikhail Bakunin's *Letters to a Frenchman* in 1870, and was further promoted by Italian, French, Russian, and other resistance movements in the 1870s. Propaganda of the deed can be summed up by a quote attributed to

Pisacane: *"ideas result from deeds, not the latter from the former, and the people will not be free when they are educated, but educated when they are free."* This idea, that direct action is more persuasive than writing or talking, has often been interpreted as recommending assassinations to awaken the public.

While deeds may sometimes result in ideas, a random act of violence will result in terror, not only in the dictatorship but also in the entire society. Terror is unlikely to inspire a society to anything except defence of their endogroup. Additionally, acts of violence will create shared guilt for the resistance and will add to the victimhood of the endo-ideal. This is more likely to create martyrs for the dictatorship than revolts against them. When the negative image is punished, it reaffirms their role as the negative image. When the endo-ideal is punished, it may be used to enhance their exceptional myth with victimhood.

Victims who commit strategic violence often strengthen their oppressors. Any cruelty or unnecessary violence by the dictatorship's opponents is likely to strengthen the dictatorship and weaken the resistance. Guilt effectively assigned to a dictator will help reshape public opinion much more effectively. By reversing the laws of endoreality, this will weaken the image of the tyrant as an endo-ideal and prevent the transfer of the tyrant's guilt to the negative image.

Ensure that guilt is assigned to the dictator. Otherwise, both guilt and punishment will be assigned to the negative image.

Step 6: Protect the vulnerable

Cruelty and oppression serve a dictatorship in several ways. In the last chapter, we discussed how shame and guilt are used to isolate people within an endogroup. A tyrant will commit atrocities, wage wars and make enemies abroad, and those external enemies will assign guilt collectively, to everyone within the endogroup. The more a dictatorship insults, threatens and attacks those outside, the more isolated and shunned the people within will become and the more they will, in turn, harden themselves against those outside. This is why it is absolutely essential to publicly and loudly resist all atrocities by the tyrant, not just those that you think personally affect you. It will all affect you, by reducing mutual empathy and connections.

A spectacle of horror creates a mesmerized public whose sole focus is on the tyrant. In the last chapter, we also discussed how guilt and shame will create social paralysis. Both of these effects make resistance appear to be impossible.

To avoid this scenario, in which the people are isolated and the dictatorship becomes impossibly strong due to social paralysis, cruelty must be vehemently resisted. The first step to this resistance is strengthening empathy with the targeted groups, which usually start with the most vulnerable in society. This nearly always starts with oppression of women, children and those outcast by legal and economic systems and cultural sectarianism. Lately, elders are frequent early victims as well. In countries where tyranny 'suddenly' appears, this empathy has almost always been eroded for decades by endemic cruelty towards the negative image. Besides the death penalty, police brutality, and other direct homicides by the state, many early victims are targeted with autogenocide.

Autogenocide is a genocide the public is coerced to commit on themselves and each other. Instead of using firing squads and death camps, this genocide is instigated by social policy and coercion. Poverty, lack of medical care, lack of housing, unhealthy food, pollution, environmental destruction, collapsing infrastructure, starvation, drugs, violence, and crime are all tools of autogenocide. It is aided by social isolation, hatred, sectarianism, and the occupation of all time, energy and resources so that people cannot or will not help each other. It includes the social coercion that encourages people to kill themselves through the instigation of chronic fear, anxiety and desperation. It uses misinformation and lack of information to prevent people from making healthy lifestyle choices. Autogenocide is instigated by entertainment that encourages violence, pornography that trains violence against women and children, social media that grows self-hatred and sectarianism, and a social and economic structure that normalizes interactions of sublation and violation instead of connection.

This is a far more widespread, pervasive and complete form of genocide than could be accomplished directly, and the hands-free nature allows those creating autogenocidal policy and coercion to reject guilt. Autogenocide is often defended by its own victims as 'freedom'. This makes the guilt easily, and sometimes automatically, transferred to the victim.

How To Dismantle a Dictatorship

The first victims of autogenocide are usually the negative images of the dominant endogroups. If the dominant endo-idealisms in a country are male, white, industrial, and wealth, the first victims will be women, non-white, unwaged, environmentalist, and poor. It is easier to transfer guilt to a negative image and convince people to ignore or encourage violence towards them since endogroups are already set up to do that.

Like many other dictatorships, the Kremlin weaponizes addiction. Russian social policies help fuel addiction which is then used to uphold totalitarianism. Anyone suffering addiction is villainized and punished, while the dissociation, fear, shame, depression, helplessness, and other social disruption caused by addiction is used to defeat resistance. Widespread addiction and the spiritual coercion of Patriarch Kirill and Putin's other accomplices and instigators in the Russian Orthodox Church are used in place of truth and healing.

Unlike most people in the US or China, who commonly adopt the roles of endo-ideal or reflector, Russians have faced such extreme repression for so long that they have been widely assigned the role of the negative image. The atrocities that Russians have endured and perpetrated for centuries have not been brought into the open and reconciled. Endoreality seems like the only safe place when truth is denied and punished and reality means facing overwhelming trauma alone. Many Russians are locked under a tyranny they will defend even as it kills them. They are in the state of emotional and social paralysis that endogroups create when they are allowed to strengthen over a long period.

A lack of solidarity is the biggest obstacle against resistance in Russia, as it is in most countries under lengthy totalitarianism. As all militaries know, drugs can be used to desensitize and dissociate people from their communities and their humanity. Shame and hatred will do the same. *Desensitization* is the creation of an endosocial barrier which empathy cannot cross. If empathy was felt, shared endogroup guilt would also immediately arrive, which is why people often prefer to be desensitized.

Desensitization is aided by identifying a group of people as the negative image. This allows their oppression to be viewed as a special case, exempt from usually accepted levels of empathy. If a man is brutally beaten by a group of men, it is shown on the news and may start an uprising in his defence. If a woman is brutally beaten by a group of men, it is shown on pornography sites with the insistence that *she likes it*. Violence is called *sex* and *love* if it happens to women or children. Slavery is called *marriage* and *adoption*. Sublation of women and children is depicted as *obedience to god*. A lack of empathy is justified through the creation of separate endoreality terms to differentiate their oppression.

As people are increasingly immersed into a predatory endogroup, they will often claim to be too busy to be aware of cruelty. Many will react angrily or talk about the stress involved in *caring about the world*. That stress is caused by guilt. People will go to any lengths to avoid guilt and its punishment, shame. Homicide, suicide, and every other form of hostility and destructive violence, at every level of society, are frequently reactions to shame. The designation of a negative image is a security that allows people to transfer their guilt instead of redeeming it through altruism and bravery.

It is a global, historical tendency of revolutionaries to want to free all men and leave them to be masters of the smallest endogroup, that of the family unit. This is reflected in the sayings *Every man is master in his own house* and *A man's home is his castle*. The lowest form of endogroup starts in the home and it forms the building block for all succeeding endogroups. Persistent misogyny, even, or especially, among revolutionary groups, is a result of a compulsion to preserve a negative image to absorb society's guilt, even while freeing everyone else.

This desire to preserve the base unit of tyranny is the seed of all other tyranny. The alternative to endogroups is *exosocialism*, which allows uninhibited expansion through relationships, discovery, creation, spirituality and other connections to sources of joy. An exosocial world cannot be built from endosocial building blocks. From the seed of misogyny and male endo-idealism, the world created every other scaled up endogroup until it resulted in state tyrannies and global empires. Just as murderers start with cruelty to animals, misogyny is the precursor and most reliable predictor of other violence against society. Terrorists begin with violence towards their mothers, wives and other women. A tyranny cannot be permanently dismantled until the negative images of every endo-idealism which upheld it are protected from sublation and violation. A dictator may be overthrown, but until the society includes the needs of everyone, including elders, children, and other different abilities, and addresses poverty, addiction, health, unwaged labour, and other sources of systemic oppression, the building blocks of dictatorship will remain.

The first step to protecting the negative image is to avoid the creation of the negative image. From *The Creation of Me, Them and Us*, the steps of negative image creation and punishment are as follows:

> *Identification*: This is a result of the endless categorization of people. It becomes most evident when a verb or adjective becomes a noun, such as *The Poor, The Disabled, The Immigrants,* or *The Homeless*. Identification is intensified if categories become an

acronym or are capitalized and start having endogroup character traits or 'culture' attributed to them. Like the endogroup itself, the negative image is an abstract concept with no basis in universal reality, so it requires an identity to exist.

Melding: There is one negative image. Disparate, or even fundamentally opposed groups are bundled under one umbrella and bear group accusations and guilt assignment. In this way, all opposition to a state or corporation can be depicted as *terrorism* if one person has been accused of a terrorist act, and one act of violence can be used to label millions of peaceful people as *violent protesters*.

Threat assignment: All negative images must be seen as a threat to the endo-ideal and the group they represent. The endogroup will insist that The Poor are after your money, The Single Mom is both a bad parent and a bad employee, The Homeless will bring down property values, The Disabled are stealing your tax dollars, and so on. The threat does not need to be consistent or correlate to any facts in universal reality. It can hold two or more opposing assertions at the same time, such as *immigrants are criminals who do not contribute to society and they are taking all the jobs*.

Guilt assignment: All guilt is assigned to the negative image and the negative image is treated as one entity where even infants are guilty of the transgressions ascribed to any member. This is obvious when children are killed in war, but it should also be apparent when children are condemned to poverty.

Curse: A curse is an otherwise meaningless word that serves to both condemn a person to the negative image and assign guilt to them for whatever bad actions are taken against them. *Illegals* is one example. A host of commonly used curses such as *bitch, slut, whore,* and new ones continually added are used to attribute guilt to women in order to justify violence against them. *DEI* is a newer curse that stands for *diversity, equity* and *inclusion*. This curse is being applied to anyone outside of the endo-ideal and assigning guilt to them for 'unjustly receiving benefits'. Curses are notable for the frequency with which they are directed at someone who is being murdered, assaulted or otherwise stripped of dignity and social rights.

Shunning: The negative image is ostracized from the rest of the endogroup in order to prevent any sympathetic or empathic connections from forming. This is increasingly happening as wealth collects into certain regions, which have a far superior living environment. It happens when women are barred from participating in some or all aspects of social life, or when children and parents are vilified for appearing in public places. Age segregation is becoming normalized in some countries, and it has led to horrific social policies and other abuse directed at elders, and sometimes children.

Punishment: Every act committed against any member of the negative image is depicted as collective punishment for the guilt assigned to the entire negative image. This is used to justify the unjustifiable, in cases such as genocide or child poverty.

Final guilt reversal for the punishment: The last stage is to transfer the guilt for their own punishment to the negative image. This continued reassignment of guilt is the root of the cyclical nature of all endosocial abuse. Persecution of people suffering from addiction, bankrupting of those suffering illness, and all the fines, charges, and jail time directed at people for not having enough money to live within the law are all ways of punishing the negative image for the endogroup's prior oppression of them.

These eight steps: identification, melding, threat assignment, guilt assignment, curse, shunning, punishment and final guilt reversal are the steps of atrocities such as genocide in Binding Chaos theory. The assignment of guilt and depiction of genocide as a collective punishment is essential in presenting a clear wrong as balanced and bypassing the tremendous guilt such an act would otherwise produce. Guilt for their own punishment is assigned to the victims to create a permanent cycle which traps them as the negative image without possibility of redemption.

IDENTIFICATION

MELDING

THREAT ASSIGNMENT

GUILT ASSIGNMENT

CURSE

SHUNNING

PUNISHMENT

FINAL GUILT REVERSAL

Genocide is an inherent part of endogroups. All endogroups have a negative image and a negative image is a genocide in the making. All of the steps above may lead to a genocide and all must be resisted as soon as they begin to form.

Do not allow guilt to be assigned unjustly. Beware of laws that only apply to a so-called *worst of the worst*. Laws must be applied equally to every person. Applying different laws to entire categories of people is the creation of a negative image. Different public reactions to violence is a sign that a negative image has already been created.

The contempt-shame symbiosis is used to transfer guilt to the negative image and the anger-fear symbiosis is used to drain energy from the negative image. Be vigilant and wary of the use of either type of interaction.

Tyranny works to destroy dignity and the components of a healthy, exosocial self, by preventing free association, violating privacy, and violating bodily autonomy. Sources of joy are destroyed, forbidden, and made inaccessible. Relationships are severed, and the ability to make connections is blocked. Discovery and creation are restricted to only the work the dictatorship requires to function. Spirituality is regulated and restricted. Guilt and shame drain the desire or ability to make new connections. These tactics all work to create a negative image.

Within an endogroup, the negative image is despised due to the laws of endoreality which assign them all guilt and shame for the group. Those outside of the endogroup are both despised and feared, as a result of an endosocial membrane and the exceptional myth. Every violation of the privacy, dignity, or safety of a negative image or outsider should be met with an immediate and forceful defensive reaction. It is these attacks that create the power structures which eventually become a dictatorship.

Successful resistance very often relies on replacing the tyrant as the centre of attention with one of their victims. This breaks the laws of endoreality by assigning guilt to the endo-ideal and removing them from the position of central focus. Jyoti Singh in India, Mohamed Bouazizi in Tunisia, Khaled Said in Egypt, Mahsa Amini and Neda Agha-Soltan in Iran, Sarah Everard in the

UK, George Floyd in the US, and others are examples where a victim, instead of being ignored like so many before them, is used as the spark for a movement for justice or a revolution. A dictatorship relies on the laws of endoreality allowing them to define who is criminal and who is shunned. Making celebrities of those they mark to be shunned and shunning those they promote as celebrities is a reversal of the endoreality which supports them.

Dictatorships rely on selfishness. They disappear people one by one with the goal of increasing isolation and callousness in those remaining. Increasing connection and solidarity is essential for resistance. Never abandon a person who has been arrested or disappeared. The regime must be made to fear arresting any one of the resistance. Every time it happens, crowds should surround police stations and politicians, and tie up every means of communication to harass those responsible until the person is released. In Serbia in the 1990s, the Otpor movement printed their famous fist logo on different coloured t-shirts, the colours symbolizing how many times the wearer had been arrested. When a person is arrested, they should be instant celebrities, with their name and image held up everywhere and a special status within the public when they are released.

The lack of connection in a dictatorship is a weakness that can be exploited and turned against the dictatorship. Never miss an opportunity to create animosity and suspicion between the tyrant and their subordinates and allies. Most people are close to someone. Nearly everyone has business associates, barbers, bakers and relatives. Target all of these connections in any way possible, and attempt to turn them against the tyrant and their supporters. Those supporting the tyrant should live in fear, isolation and suspicion, in every aspect of their lives.

Think of basic social coercion, the kind that happens in small towns or schools. What happens when a child acts out in school? The school calls their parents. Other children tell their parents. The other parents treat the first parents to stares and raised eyebrows. The first parents experience shame. They are strongly motivated to try to change their child's behaviour. Create a situation where every member of a tyranny has a social network that is ashamed of the association and motivated to convince them to change their behaviour. They should not be able to escape accusation by going home or on holidays. Charge a very high price for oppression, a price the dictator and their henchmen cannot afford.

REFUSE LABELS	REJECT COLLECTIVE GUILT	REJECT FEAR
DETERMINE GUILT	RECLAIM DIGNITY	CREATE CONNECTIONS
DOCUMENT & RESIST	REFUSE TO BLAME VICTIMS	

Your goal is to reverse and remove the endoreality that creates the dictatorship's negative image. Recognize and support anyone the dictatorship casts as the negative image; remove recognition and support from their endo-ideal. Reassign guilt and shame from their negative image to their endo-ideal. Do not allow any of the steps of negative image creation.

Tyranny survives on sublation and violation. Connection is the domain of resistance. Solidarity is a strength the resistance has over the dictatorship.

How To Dismantle a Dictatorship

Step 7: Cultivate external allies

Thailand's dissolute, 72-year-old king, Rama X, has lived in Germany for many years, along with his large entourage. I was in Thailand during his 3-day coronation, where he and his fourth wife briefly appeared for a parade and a balcony wave. His giant, extremely photoshopped image was plastered throughout Bangkok during the one billion baht ceremony. Despite the pomp and expense, he shows no interest in Thailand or its people beyond using the country as his personal piggy bank to fund his opulent and debauched lifestyle in Germany. He refuses to cede power to a regent to represent him in his permanent absence and instead, empowers a de facto military dictatorship. In his absence, the Thai military enforces brutal lèse-majesté laws to punish any criticism of the royal family.

Rama X receives diplomatic immunity in Germany as a head of state, but he does little to warrant the appellation besides strengthening the monarchy and ordering ruthless oppression of democracy activists and journalists. Instead, he throws extravagant parties to mark occasions such as the birthday of his poodle, Foo Foo. He used his position as the head of the Royal Thai Armed Forces to appoint Foo Foo as a chief marshal in the Thai Air Force before Foo Foo died and received a lavish, four-day funeral.

Many European and North American states allow dictators and oligarchs around the world to enrich themselves and their hosts with wealth stolen from their home countries. Like the others, Germany has no particular motivation to stop hosting this degenerate tyrant. Rama X is oppressing his own people, but he siphons their money into Germany to maintain amusements such as his private fleet of 38 aircraft, including a Boeing 737. If you want to overthrow your dictator, and you happen to be Thai, you need to create alliances in Germany and gain their assistance in removing the profligate libertine from power.

Even if your dictator is a stay-at-home, like Bashar al-Assad, Recep Tayyip Erdogan, or Muammar Gaddafi, they will be upheld by other states whose objectives are in opposition to yours. While Assad was posing as the enemy of the west and Israel, the US was outsourcing victims to his torture prisons. Israel propped up Assad during the Syrian revolution, and they have been bombing the fledgling democracy which replaced him since it took power. Russian military assisted Assad's genocide of Syrians for most of the war. Erdogan is propped up by many supposed democracy advocates, as was Gaddafi, for similar reasons: the undemocratic state provides strong regional 'stability'. In Gaddafi's case, Libya acted as a cork in the bottle separating sub-Saharan refugees from Europe, and Middle Eastern guns and gunmen from Africa. In Erdogan's case, he is sometimes seen as the counter to Israeli / Russian dominance in the Middle East and has negotiated tactical agreements with both. In both cases, lives within the country are ignored to protect lives or lifestyles outside the country.

Political leaders are accountable to those they represent. Few foreign politicians are going to support you in taking down your dictator if it endangers their own stability or prosperity.

They may even work against you. Tyrants are usually kept in power by complicity with other states who hide their stolen money, allow them to live in luxury while the people starve, and aid and abet their eventual flights from justice.

Resistance to a dictatorship often needs external recognition and support to survive. At the very least, you need other countries to not provide military and other aid to your oppressor. Hopefully, other countries will also provide humanitarian assistance, allow refugees, and pressure the dictator to ease repression. If you successfully remove the dictatorship, you are even more likely to require external support as your new government will need recognition from neighbours and trading partners to continue joint operations.

Anyone facing international strengthening of their dictators needs international support to counter it. Appealing directly to the people and journalists in other countries may have some effect. Eventually, however, the most effective strategy is to convince foreign rulers that you too will be able to provide stability, and show them your plan for doing so. Especially in cases of regional strongmen like Gaddafi and Erdogan, such a plan is absolutely necessary if you do not want allied countries to intervene in the name of 'stability'.

In many countries, dictators are upheld because they protect or provide lucrative contracts to multinational and foreign corporations. The 18 years that Joseph Kabila was president of the Democratic Republic of Congo, and the preceding nearly four years that his father was president, were marked by resource contracts which can only be described as pillaging and looting the country. The DRC, which ought to be one of the wealthiest countries on earth based on natural resources, has been the victim of contracts signed with Kabila's very best friend, Israeli Dan Gertler. Gertler has operated a pipeline that siphoned money out of the DRC and into Israel and elsewhere, since 1997. In exchange, he upheld his presidential partner-in-crime.

Like Samsung in South Korea, corporations often wield more power and have more impunity than politicians. In the United States, an evolving acronym is used to represent the most powerful technology companies. The latest version is GAMAM, for Google, Amazon, Meta, Apple and Microsoft. Some shorten that to MAGA, Meta/Microsoft, Apple, Google, Amazon, to represent the companies' outsized influence over the current governance of the US. Many corporations, such as Nestle, have been permitted impunity to act as global super villains for decades with no repercussions. Smaller and poorer countries are especially susceptible to threats and bribes from these marauding pillagers dictating their government policies and appointing leaders to act in their interests.

In countries accustomed to acting as global endo-ideals, people tend to be less aware of why influence or opinions of them outside their borders matter. Sometimes, external opinions really do not make much difference, but usually, they do. How much they matter depends on what the state's power is based on.

Russia is an empire based on its control of more than one ninth of the land in the world. China is an empire because it controls more than 17% of the people in the world. The US is an endo-ideal because the world made it an endo-ideal. The US was internationally revered as a potential political utopia, first, when it was colonized and second, when it gained independence. Since then, it has increased its power because of the world's reflection. Currently, the US exists as a global power largely because of the world's opinion of them. As reflectors, most of the rest of the world benefits from US strength and would suffer if it collapsed overnight, but reflectors can create new relationships and gradually build strength elsewhere. If that were to happen, US power could be largely dismantled based on external disapproval.

The *approval economy* is a concept from the *Binding Chaos* series. Even China and Russia are very susceptible to the world's approval, as we have seen in the impact of sanctions on Russia. I have been warning for decades that the US is very vulnerable because US power is so dependent on *vapour capital* and *vapour wealth*, capital and wealth based on nothing but international approval.

Around 40% of US GDP relies heavily on the demand that the world obey their draconian 'intellectual property' laws in industries such as technology, pharmaceuticals and entertainment. Intellectual property is a concept. As such, it can disappear as soon as the world says, *The emperor has no clothes.* Every other country in the world would see a net benefit from a reduction in intellectual property laws. The world agrees to recognize these laws for no reason other than approval granted to the US. What would happen if the world stopped recognizing US intellectual property? The US would lose dominance in most areas and would lose entire major industries outright.

US bonds are used as a platinum credit card that allows the US to borrow very large amounts of money at low interest rates; 33% of that debt is held outside the US. This money is used as capital to develop US industry, innovation and military power. US financial security depends on this credit and the stability of the US dollar. The US dollar is stable because the world agrees to uphold its stability. What happens if external debt and currency holders divest of their holdings? US debt would be perceived as risky and buyers will demand a higher rate of return to invest in it. That means more interest will be required for the US to continue its lifestyle. Eventually, the US could default on their debt and the US economy could tank, with fallout such as pension defaults and skyrocketing inflation. This would destroy their credit rating and make it very unlikely they would be given access to an unlimited platinum credit card again.

The US is the money laundering capital of the world. They allow secret corporations to hide wealth stolen from other countries, they offer corporate tax havens to encourage foreign corporations to locate there, and they create easy money laundering opportunities through NGOs, stocks, cryptocurrency, overpriced real estate, supercars, art and the other usual money laundering assets. The US is the country that harbours the most shell companies and hidden assets. At the same time, the US has strongarmed nearly every other country into acting as a global surveillance system preventing any money from leaving the US. FATCA, the Foreign Account Tax Compliance Act, requires every other signatory state to interrogate customers on behalf of the US and look for any money the US may feel entitled to. Other countries are upholding an attempted US monopoly on money laundering.

This has made the US the beneficiary of money stolen from countries around the world, but especially from countries with already fragile economies. All of this money could move out if the US becomes totalitarian and a high risk economy. This would cause crashes in all the areas foreign money usually sits, like real estate, luxury cars, artwork and all their related industries. If other countries refuse to comply with FATCA, money could start pouring out of the US instead.

80% of US population increases comes from immigration. That immigration includes significant contributors in innovation, research, sports, entertainment, and other industry-developing fields. Without global approval, the US will no longer be able to claim the top talent and innovations in the world as their own. The brain drain that other countries have experienced has benefited the US for decades. Now, the US could experience their own brain drain but, more importantly, they will cease to benefit from others. Without global talent, entire US industries would be greatly diminished. Along with the talent, the interest in the US as the global endo-ideal is a huge part of their marketing. Tourism and entertainment are just two areas that depend entirely on the world's fascination with the US.

Some US exports are products that they force the rest of the world to purchase as 'diplomacy', another power that is dependent on global approval. If the world ignores US threats, US corporations will lose sales and overseas expansion that other countries have been forced to accept against their own best interests. Speaking of diplomacy, US political power is based on shared resources with other countries, including both military and intelligence. If other countries stop providing the US with critical information, the US will be left with huge dark areas in knowledge they need to protect themselves domestically and internationally. If US military is forced to withdraw from foreign bases, that will leave US corporations vulnerable in foreign countries. In addition, the foreign aid the US relies on in times of natural disasters such as forest fires could be greatly diminished. Even goods and services traded to the US could be impacted, as premium trade goods are offered to favoured trading partners. Less favoured states do not have the same access to products that the US currently enjoys.

Diplomacy, debt, and intellectual property are all vapour capital and vapour wealth. They are just manifestations of the world's approval. When the approval disappears, so does the entire structure of supposed wealth. The US is not the only example of this. Nearly every billionaire has been elevated on the same precarious bubble of vapour wealth, and 30% of the world's billionaires live in the US. Because the US economy is so dependent on the international approval economy, a removal of approval would collapse them as a global power.

What would such a collapse mean for a potential internal conflict? A power structure is a vicious cycle, requiring ever-increasing levels of violence. An extreme endogroup will either increase the oppression of its own negative image to intolerable levels (North Korea, Syria under the Assad family) or it will expand its negative image (Russia, Israel) or both. The US has so far taken its worst aggression outside its borders. If it is driven back by the rest of the world, the people within the country will begin to experience far greater oppression. We are already seeing totalitarian repercussions on anyone attempting to leave or return to the US, as well as militarized borders. Borders with Canada and Mexico are being strengthened by the US and also by Canada and Mexico. Ostensibly, this is to keep people out of the US, but it will be used to keep them in, as well. Even with open borders, Russians have found themselves increasingly unwelcome outside of Russia due to their complicity with Kremlin crimes. Isolation strengthens the endogroup and increases internal oppression.

There are many reasons for people trapped within an increasingly predatory dictatorship to start creating international goodwill now. Alliances can provide help by lobbying their own governments to cut ties with your dictator, or by providing practical aid. Outside relationships also help to weaken endogroups by reducing the focus on the dictator and the control the dictatorship has over all aspects of life.

International advocates are also essential after your tyrant is removed. The world historically holds all citizens responsible for any external crimes their countries have committed and debt owed by their country. Debt results in imposed austerity measures that keep citizens impoverished for decades and may cripple their economic future for generations. Everyone is punished for the crimes of their governments. If your resistance is not internationally networked, recognized, and respected, you will face collective punishment.

Both France and Thailand benefited, at least partially, from the prominent resistance and external alliances of the French Resistance and the Free Thai Movement when World War II reparations were calculated. Recently in Syria, and currently in Burma, the resistance movements are also prominent. Many people in both places resisted to the point of years-long civil war. It is undeniable that they are separate from their dictator, and nothing more could reasonably be asked of them. Any shared guilt they may have been assigned was atoned long ago. Additionally, the Syrian and Burmese militaries were focused on internal oppression, so there was not much guilt to be attributed for external crimes.

Countries like Russia are a very different case. When external aggression has occurred, debt must be paid. No one asks who anyone in the country voted for when war reparations are due. They don't ask when assets are seized, and they don't ask when bombs are dropped. Endogroup retribution is applied to the entire endogroup. The only hope of avoiding this retribution lies in a complete and final separation from the tyrant's endogroup. A region that breaks off and successfully declares early independence may be exempt. Anyone that still looks affiliated is not.

For all of these reasons, it is very important to differentiate your resistance from the tyranny and establish yourself as the people's rightful representative, as we discussed in *Step 1*. Resist any attempt to recognize the dictatorship as a valid representative with any authority to negotiate. Discourage foreign or local regional governments or businesses from negotiating with the tyrant. Be very clear that any deals signed with the tyrant will not be respected and will be legally void when they are overthrown. An external party is not going to oust your tyrant for you, however. The only way to stop external negotiations is to put up real resistance and ensure that such deals cannot effectively be implemented. If you don't want your tyrant's partners to retaliate, you have to provide them with an alternate power to negotiate with as soon as possible. Try to create regional bodies to negotiate with outsiders and undermine the government's authority.

Allies in other countries are essential to counter external recognition of your dictator. Recognition from the United Nations is often not reflective of public opinion. UN recognition can be effectively replaced by recognition of the people. People outside can support your resistance with mass boycotts to crash your country's economy, online support, education and counter propaganda, and pressure on their own governments and corporations to isolate your tyrant. An endo-ideal needs external recognition from their peers to exist externally as an endo-ideal. Do everything you can to block external recognition of the dictator. Do everything you can to achieve external recognition for the resistance.

Isolate the tyrant.

Discourage anyone from recognizing the tyrant as a legitimate ruler or upholding them.

Build relationships with people outside of your country and work to be able to negotiate with their heads of state and corporations.

Step 8: Take the focus

The hyperfocus of an endogroup on an endo-ideal is what creates the endo-ideal. The endo-ideal is a spectacle that occupies the minds of the people. Dictators are addicted to airtime. Without this hyperfocus, the dictator loses the power to control the daily lives of the public.

In a power relationship, one person acts and the other reacts. A dictator issues anger; the public responds with fear. The dictator issues contempt; the public reacts with shame. The one who acts has power over the reactions of the other. In this way, they control the other's emotions and can manipulate the unconscious emotional responses that we talked about in *Step 2*. In order to take the focus, the resistance must be the one that acts.

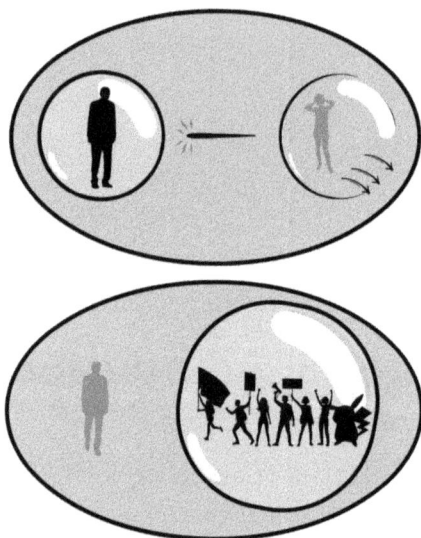

Instead of waiting for and focusing on oppression of the people by the tyrants, create scenarios where the tyrant must actively resist the will of the people. Cause them stress, put them in danger and occupy their thoughts every day. When the tyrant uses fear and anger or contempt and shame in an attempt to sublate the public, turn it on them. To return to the Trump – Zelensky spectacle from *Step 5*, the purpose of attacking Zelensky's clothes and manners was to humiliate him personally. The public retaliated by turning his primary attacker into a meme to ridicule him with wherever he went. This is turning contempt and shame back to the aggressor. Anger and fear can be responded to in the same way. As the regime terrorizes the public with videos of street abductions, imprisonment and death, the response should be reminders of previous tyrants as what will happen to them eventually.

A dictatorship can fill media and institutions with its brands, including the face of the dictator, the stolen flag and symbols of national identity. Resistance needs its own symbols. A resistance movement can flood streets and public places with their symbols far more extensively than the regime can. The stylized fist of the Serbian resistance, spray painted everywhere, or the roses of the Georgian Rose Revolution or the yellow umbrellas and ribbons of Hong Kong's resistance movement, are emotionally evocative symbols that can be posted everywhere from streets to online avatars. Singing anthems like Bella Ciao, or using them as ringtones, flashing the three fingered salute, and banging pots are ways to express solidarity or resistance in everyday life. When the symbols of resistance crowd out the symbols of the dictatorship, it is evident to all that the dictator has lost control of the people and is no longer the focus of the country. If they are not the focus, they are not the endo-ideal.

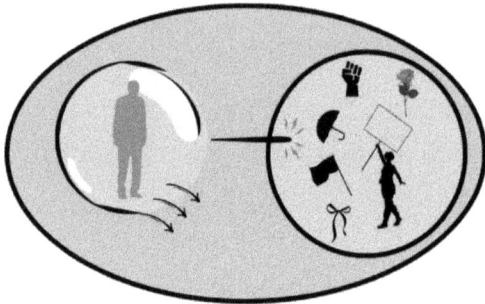

Cataloguing crimes and other actions of a regime is very important. Obsessing over them to the exclusion of all else is self-defeating. It is not necessary for every pundit to produce their own analysis of everything the tyranny does, and it is not necessary for people to read and watch everything from or about the tyranny. Occupied people that incessantly repeat everything the occupier says or does are emotionally acting as reflectors, even if they consciously oppose the tyrant. The more their attention vectors towards the endo-ideal, the more fear and shame they experience, and the more blind and uncaring they become to the negative image and those outside the endogroup. At some point, critics of a dictatorship are enabling its hold on power by giving it the full spotlight. Your task is to bring the spotlight onto the resistance.

Just as television brought the conflicts of the 1960s into people's living rooms, the internet brought the conflicts of the 2000's to people's fingertips. It is hard to imagine the years from 2008 to 2012 without the online tools of revolutionaries and resistance. We used mailing lists, collaborative pads and VPNs from Riseup, forums, task boards, and other social networking tools from lorea / n-1.cc, Jabber/xmpp for encrypted chats, and IRC for large hangouts. Many new whistleblowing and leak platforms helped expose crimes and corruption and encouraged a generation of activist hackers. Our collective media was my own *Wikileaks Central* and others like *Roar* magazine. People streamed protests on Ustream or Bambuser, often on popular channels like Tomalatele or Peoplewitness. We held virtual assemblies on Mumble and dropped public links to leaks and manifestos on Pastebin. We dreamed of alternatives to hierarchical corporations with Bettermeans for project management. Loomio arose later from the need for tools for collaborative decision making. My own Getgee, originally Global Square, was designed as an open and collaborative alternative to the world wide web and the hierarchy and algorithmic control of social media. It was all part of this exciting new ecosystem we were creating to structure a different way of living.

Marshall McLuhan was accurate for his time in 1960 when he said, *"The medium is the message,"* but he was even more prescient in describing mine. The tools themselves were revolutionary and powerful. They made us exciting and interesting, to the media and to those who joined. For the first time, the audience was participating instead of passively watching; they were part of the protests and the revolutions. They could bring a battery if a streamer needed one or open a wifi hotspot for people in the street below. The Translator Brigades used collaborative pads to turn out high speed translations of manifestos, news and other circulars, and we used the same pads for collaborative writing. What we produced on our own tools was then dropped somewhere so it could be picked up and broadcast by the new soon-to-be-influencers on Twitter and Youtube. From these initial collaborative tools, we produced a generation of independent media outlets, streamers, writers, websites, and even new political parties, such as Podemos in Spain.

The new technologies didn't just report revolutions; they enabled them. Resistance was deeply shaped by decentralized media and networked coordination tools that bypassed traditional hierarchies. Having our own tools allowed us to tell our own stories, bypass corporate media narratives, and coordinate globally in real time. It allowed us to respond to attacks effectively and immediately.

I have heard people complain that corporate media used to cover protests more, but it's not true. Yes, they covered Egypt's Tahrir Square protests, but that is only because they almost completely missed the Tunisian revolution. Most didn't start covering that until Ben Ali was deposed, and then they wrote articles with titles like, *What is Tunisia and why does it matter?*" It was our online ecosystem of mutual support that forced media coverage and, at the same time, made it less relevant.

Almost none of this ecosystem exists now. By 2010, centralized social media accounts had taken off and were taking up increasingly more time and attention. I developed a workaround for social media decentralization for a time: I would write a package containing an explanatory video, a Pastebin press release for media, a Pastebin of social media posts with an accompanying hashtag, and a countdown clock for the start. Everyone would send the prewritten posts at the same time and continue over the next hours and days to create and maintain a global trend. These *tweetstorms* were very popular because they provided free, well-written and researched posts that were likely to get a lot of interaction for social media users. Instead of being critcized for stealing others work, they were credited with altruism while building clout. Soon, the social media algorithms made this tactic less effective as well. If our tools were a large part of our movements, the co-option of our tools was a large part of our demise.

Even by 2010, the influence of state coercion agencies, especially Russian, was pervasive in alternate media. Since then, their messaging has flooded streamers, social media, podcasts, videos, and forums of all sizes. Youtube's algorithm used to be notable for the blatant grooming of its audiences, especially men, towards misogyny and other extremist violence. Now this is a feature of most large platforms. From porn sites to reddit to Tumblr to Twitter and Meta, abusive content that was once restricted to chan boards is the mainstream. At the same time, thought bubbles, created by platform fragmentation and the algorithms, have greatly increased polarization. Disinformation, aided by 'artificial intelligence', has made people much more suspicious of news outside what they are already familiar with. Financial incentives, bots and the algorithms have flooded platforms with advertising and state and corporate coercion. Group chats are now the strategizing tools of choice and they are, like all the broadcast platforms, inherently hierarchical.

These circumstances are a result of a lack of interest and labour. It has never been easier to create our own tools and spaces, both online and offline. We need to reawaken the use and development of tools that encourage collaboration and avoid hierarchy and co-option. We need to recreate an ecosystem of verified, trustworthy knowledge. We need to replace opinions from 'artificial intelligence' and influencers with genuine expertise, which is seldom found in the chronically online or the populist podcast regulars. Influencers should be working as knowledge bridges, transparently amplifying and breaking down information from verified research. This is not a difficult ecosystem to create.

We need effective online tools, but if they are just going to be used to share news of dictators, we may as well stay on the old. Online tools are only revolutionary if they are used to create communities and resistance. Abandoning the tyrant's tools is only the first step; we also have to abandon their narratives. Force their media to react to the resistance by making the resistance all people are talking about. Once you have taken the audience focus, people will not watch media that does not cover your actions.

Initially, this requires actions that are so outrageous, awe-inspiring, or funny that people will discuss them for days. In the long term, your news will be the most watched and read if it is the most relevant to people's lives and future. In the early 2000s, this focus was often achieved through leaks; we were giving people information they trusted that they could not get anywhere else. Now, people need a direction for their future, which is why that has been my primary focus for the last decade, since 2015.

If your focus remains on the dictator, your best outcome is the removal of the dictator, after which your movement will go home, and a new dictator will be back in a day or a year. A driver will drive into an object they are staring at. A public will attain the future they are focused on. Clear your mind of thoughts of the tyrants, and replace them with your vision of the future. The image that you want in your head, and the heads of others, is the better future you dream of.

As soon as you remove your focus from the dictator to yourselves, you will see that so much needs to be built. How do we want to be governed? What do we want our communities to look like? How will we address our current and future challenges such as climate change? What better solutions can we create for the financial system, knowledge, community structures like transportation, housing and food? What should our legal system look like? So many discussions, so much creation, so many decisions, so much action. As long as this is organized well enough that it is not overwhelming, it will be fascinating and exciting and much more interesting than any stale old dictator.

People under totalitarianism are miserable and without hope. In this state, they are very open to a vision of the future that offers an escape through their imaginations. Once they have bonded to that vision, they will fight for it as anyone will fight for their only source of hope and joy. If you can replace the fear of the unknown with excitement for the future, you will successfully take the focus from the dictator. Once the focus is on the alternative, energy will build for the alternative. You will need this energy because once the tyrant is removed, you still have to dismantle the tyranny, brick by brick and debate after debate. Removing the tyrant is only the first battle.

Taking the focus from the dictator requires the creation of a resistance that inspires public trust and excitement. It is not enough to fight against something; to be inspired, people need to be fighting for something.

Step 9: Create the alternative

Revolution after revolution tries to follow the script of movies, legends and fairy tales. Kill the bad guy, they teach, and the villagers will be joyful and live in peace. In the real world, if a government is toppled without an alternative in its place, society can collapse overnight. The death and destruction brought by a lack of infrastructure has frequently been worse than the violence during a revolution. In *Step 1*, I mentioned that revolutions can act as a trigger for extreme nationalism. This is because traumatized populations bond to strong endogroups. People coming out of a revolution need security and a clear path ahead. Never weed without planting.

The 2010-2011 resistance movements in Tunisia, Egypt, Libya, and Yemen had one goal: *The people demand the fall of the regime.* They were all very successful at achieving that goal. Understandably, achieving it required singular focus and limited time to agree on much besides a short list of demands. After the primary goal was achieved, they have all struggled with the aftermath. Dictatorships that are toppled with limited structure prepared to catch the collapsing nation have three paths open to them: they can scale up as part of a transcendental empire, meaning they will be under foreign dominance, they can collapse down into earlier sectarian factions, or they can put a new figurehead on the old structure. In any of these cases, they are very likely to find themselves under a tyrant again. Avoiding all of these familiar and easier paths to chart a new direction while living in a collapsed society is very difficult.

The long series of events sometimes referred to collectively as the French Revolution is a prominent example of what happens when a dictatorship is collapsed with no alternative ready. In 59 years, France had three major revolutions. The one properly called the French Revolution is the first, which was fought from

1789 to 1792 to overthrow Louis the XVI. As soon as the king was dead, the country fell into a bloodbath called the Reign of Terror, until the leader of that, Maximilien de Robespierre, was killed in 1794. This was followed by a coup and a new king, Napoléon Bonaparte, who quickly declared himself emperor. Napoléon involved France in a bloody tangle of external wars during his rule from 1804 to 1814. In 1814, France brought another king, Louis XVIII, back from exile. This one was in power for ten years, except for the 100 days when Napoléon came back from exile. By 1830, France was again tired enough of the monarchy to have another revolution. This time, they forced the sitting King Charles X to abdicate and installed a 'citizen king'. The third revolution was in 1848, after which they appointed a president who happened to be the nephew of their former emperor, Napoléon. The nephew promptly conducted a political coup and made himself an emperor, Napoléon III. In addition to the three revolutions, this period was marked by much more unrest, such as the 1832 rebellion immortalized in *Les Misérables*.

It took three revolutions and 59 years of strife, misery, death, and continual resistance for France to overthrow a king and end up with an emperor. They would not see a lasting republic until their third attempt, in 1870. There is a reason so much French literature is devoted to philosophy of governance and political theory. They tested new theory repeatedly, in their government and colonies, in the Paris Commune in 1871, and in what they idealistically called The New World. They started long before the first revolution and continue to this day. Besides the fact that they were fighting a proxy war with England, French people enthusiastically supported and aided the United States liberation in 1776 because they also were searching for freedom from tyranny. The French are now on the fifth iteration of their republic, and clearly, they are still working on it.

Many people reference the French Revolution as though some people just stormed the Bastille, cut off some heads and voila, France was a democracy. The real history reflects the effort truly required to create a better alternative. It requires forethought, wide and deep communication, and continual participation. French history reflects the need to experiment, re-examine and iterate with new solutions. We cannot just create a system of governance and leave it unexamined for centuries while we change everything else about society. It must be stable but not rigid, able to respond to new threats without retreating to old mistakes, and hold to principles while remaining flexible with methods. Governance is an action. It is a living, breathing institution that is a part of everyone living under it.

A revolution cannot wait for a complete map forward, but it must have guiding principles for the future so that people do not collapse into ideological wars after the tyrant is deposed. A complete parallel government cannot usually be created during a revolution, but some institutions will have to be created if the revolution is to survive. Dismantling a government is ideally like a snake shedding its skin, or a turtle the outer scutes of its shell. The replacement is created while the old still exists, and the old just flakes off when it is no longer being used. A society is still vulnerable with a new government, but not as vulnerable as they would be with no government at all.

At the least, a revolutionary movement must have principles, plans and procedures. These have different requirements for development. If your new community is not to repeat mistakes of history, you will need people who understand history to create your principles and explain why they are the best choice for your future. These people will need to understand what conditions created the dictatorship in the first place and what needs to be done to ensure it isn't recreated. They must understand the legal and political principles followed by other states that you wish to ally with or gain recognition from. They should understand international law and be familiar with bills of rights and constitutions from many countries so they can make the best recommendations. Most of all, they need to understand what problems the people in the country are facing and what principles would protect them from their current suffering.

Principles may seem esoteric and a trivial waste of time to those fighting in the streets. As countries like Syria have learned, the principles you endorse, or fail to endorse, can have a great impact on your success both during and after your revolution. Syrians simply wanted rid of Assad. They wanted to live a life free from daily terror and oppression. The revolution was a surprise, an increasingly broad opposition to increasingly public atrocities. The resistance did not initially have the time or the foreign coaching to help them perfect an image to present to the world; they were trying to stay alive.

Assad had been depicted outside of Syria for years as the most secular option for Syrian leadership, so it was easy for his regime and Kremlin backers to flood international media with claims that the ordinary people he was murdering were *religious extremists*. This isolated the budding revolution to the point that the only allies willing to come to their assistance were religious extremists. Assad's propaganda was self-fulfilling. Principles are very important to have ready for the first event that receives international media coverage. If you don't define yourself, your enemy will. Once you are labelled, media tends to cut and paste that labelling into every story thereafter, and it can be very hard to shake off, especially if it becomes self-fulfilling. Ukraine faced the same Kremlin propaganda machine depicting them all as *nazis* during the initial Russian invasion in 2014, but by the time of the full-scale invasion in 2022, they and international allies were much more prepared to counter the labelling with clear principles and their own narrative.

It is necessary to agree on a few overall principles before or during a revolution, both for image control and to ensure there is no immediate ideological war following the collapse of the dictator. The primary concerns of the public following a revolution are not principles, however. People will want to know where the police are and who their allegiance is to. They need to know where food is coming from and where the children will go to school. They need roads repaired and buses running on time. Principles are not enough; you also need plans.

A common principle for revolutions is *democracy*. This needs more specific detail before anyone can implement that, or imagine it. The principles are an important starting point, but they may only make sense to some people as specific outcomes. To build agreement for the large goal, it usually has to be broken down into bite sized goals. Lofty principles need relatable application in daily life. Taxes on salt and tea are sometimes more concrete than life without the dictator. We may want to end autogenocide, but we can start with protests against contaminated food. Resistance spreads as people become able to envision what the desired outcome would mean in their own lives.

You need to plan a road from where you are to your goal. You don't want oligarchy, okay. What are the rules to keep oligarchy from influencing your first election and controlling your first institutions? Your future vision includes communities that care for each other and don't allow anyone to suffer needlessly, okay. What is your plan for when your neighbour is seriously injured and all hospitals and clinics are destroyed or closed to you? What will you do for food security and securing essential items? What are your alternatives for transport?

Plans detail exactly what your resistance movement will do to resist while continuing to ensure safety and survival as much as possible. The Syrian White Helmets, or Syria Civil Defence, were one of the first resistance cohorts established in Syria. These skilled and brave volunteers helped people prepare for and deal with the aftermath of Assad's genocidal attacks on civilians. They taught preparation, performed search and rescue operations in the aftermath of bombings, and evacuated civilians. Because of their effectiveness and bravery, and because their work was in such opposition to the Assad/Kremlin depiction of Syrian resistance, they were a constant target of disinformation campaigns. Although these campaigns depicted them as foreign-funded propagandists, they were civilians who responded to attacks as neighbours and learned along the way. They started to receive some foreign training and financial aid as they became more organized and adopted a principle of humanitarian impartiality.

MSF, or Doctors Without Borders, is an international organization that is present in over

70 countries and is also, by far, my favourite NGO. Since 1971, MSF has provided medical care around the world, especially in conflict zones and places with ineradicable disease. It is notable how often they are the last to leave a conflict zone and the first to alert the world to new disease outbreaks. MSF is not just a team of medical professionals; they also provide invaluable data and testimony regarding disease and conflicts. They contribute a great deal to the establishment of local medical services and training of medical professionals in areas that lack medical care. They are an organization, but they act much more like a movement, with their own principles. Professionally, they are like a global version of the Kallawaya, the traditional, travelling healers of Bolivia.

The reason I am bringing up MSF is because they provide an alternative to expecting people in disasters, including revolutions, to immediately learn to do everything themselves from scratch. It is possible to create alliances with people who have the networks and knowledge to help you establish what you need. The time to reach out to create those connections is immediately, preferably long before a revolution starts.

And once you have all of your plans, what then? Well, now you need actions. Plans are great, but even the most detailed plan needs a first action to be taken. Your procedure outlines how, when and who should take that action. Moving from principles to plans to procedures should be a smooth transition that creates a seamless and unified image. This will help you to gain the public confidence you need for people to trust and align with the resistance. If you try to omit any of those steps, people will be justly wary to put faith in your resistance. If you want people to join you in an action, but you are noncommittal on whether your end goal is a democracy, a theocracy or an experimental anarchy, they will be wary of joining you. If you say you want to establish peace, but your methods include a massacre, your audience will, hopefully, reject you. If you change your principles, or neglect to change your procedures, you will very likely fail.

Once you have your principles and your plans, your procedures can be as flexible and dynamic as they need to be, as long as they do not contradict the principles or sabotage the plans. If your plans include alliances with international networks like MSF or journalists, your procedures had better not attack them or their allies. If your principles include working justice systems, you had better not assassinate your enemies without trials, or give them amnesty. You aren't just trying to survive; you are establishing a unified national identity.

Aligned principles, plans and procedures are all essential for a resistance to inspire public trust and interest and remove the focus from the dictatorship.

You will need to train and establish the services that are or may be required. There is no one blueprint for this as countries are unique in what infrastructure collapses and what challenges they face. Broadly, you will need guardians who defend communities, and caretakers who support communities. You should have an initial plan for what types of personal, neighbourhood, and national defence will be best suited to your situation and train people to be ready for that. This may have to include physical defence, but it is much better if that defence can be as nonviolent as possible and includes legal and international lobbying. This is where you need your alternate media established, legal volunteers and external allies. Your caretakers are those who will supplement medical care, food, education, shelter, disaster response, and any other infrastructure that may be disrupted. They will need to be networked with other communities for rapid response and resilience, and they too will need international allies.

You will need:

Alternate media.

Legal volunteers.

International allies.

Community infrastructure.

Community networks.

Transportation.

Communication.

Other defence apparatus.

How To Dismantle a Dictatorship

Some form of alternative governance must be created while the revolution is still ongoing if you want to establish relationships with external states and corporations. That governance may be set up as transitional or as a party that hopes to be permanent. Even if future governance is left to the future, it is a good idea to create the criteria that any new government will have to fulfill. If you have the criteria, you can persuade future, or even current candidates to agree to the terms in the hope of avoiding the election of new tyrants.

This all requires a lot of coordination between people who may not initially have anything in common other than a desire to overthrow a dictator. The amount of communication required is a difficult task under oppression and surveillance. You can circumvent the dictatorship by establishing autonomous regions, government in exile, underground government, or all three.

The first step to setting up your resistance government is to hold neighbourhood and community meetings and discuss what is required from this government. This is where you develop and evolve your principles, plans and procedures. Initial questions include:

Who will participate and how is participation facilitated?

Are decisions by majority vote, consensus, or other criteria such as expertise?

Are you including external networks and allies in your resistance plans?

Is your resistance going to be fully unified or a coalition of autonomous groups or regions?

What expertise and resources do you have and what do you still need for both guardianship and caretaking?

The first challenge is establishing lines of communication and ensuring they remain open. Here, external allies can be very valuable. If you have trusted networks you can get information to, they can pass it on or broadcast it to your audience. If many people have fled the country, they can be very useful in lobbying on your behalf and in setting up external support networks. Reach beyond the familiar, to people unaffiliated with your country as well. Do not just regret the loss of allies as your state aligns with other despots. Create and refuse to relinquish external bonds and relationships. Read and talk to those outside. Form economic ties with them, even where it becomes difficult. Do not simply ask for or demand assistance when it is urgent; build real relationships and start early. Be generous in your relationships so that people are willing to return your generosity when you need it.

This book is about how to dismantle a dictatorship. *How to Build Community During Conflict* is the name of another book in the *Resistance* series, so I am not going into too much more detail about it here. They are integrally related, however. If you haven't created a healthy and supportive community, then you may have gotten rid of a dictator, but you have not dismantled the dictatorship. At the beginning of this chapter, I said *Never weed without planting.* As you weed out the elements of a dictatorship, plant a healthy community. That is how you prevent a dictatorship from growing again.

Endogroups are created from fear and guilt. Dictatorships need to create fear and allocate guilt to a negative image in order to form. Resistance against dictatorships means preventing situations where populations are kept in chronic fear and processing guilt properly when it arises. With the power structure dismantled, no one acting as reflectors to deny and create reality and police the population, guilt properly assigned, no negative image to be punished for the guilt of others, and no recognition of the tyrant as an endo-ideal, you have only a person, or a small cabal, to contend with. With a viable alternative structure of guardians and caretakers for people to transition to, the defensive support has left the dictatorship. Now, finally, the tyrants are just people. Arrest them.

The people demand the fall of the regime.

Ash-sha'b yurīd isqāṭ an-niẓām الشعب يريد إسقاط النظام,

How To Dismantle a Dictatorship

Afterword

There are many more initial questions that will need to be addressed by a resistance movement, such as: *How do I start a mass movement against tyranny? How do I survive the collapse of the power structure I have been living under? How do I resist and combat coercion? How do I build a community during conflict?* These questions and more are explored in other books in the *Resistance* series, a practical set of guides which each address specific goals.

As a series of short and specific guides, the *Resistance* series leaves out theory and supporting research for the ideas they are built on. If you want to know more about endogroups, roles, guilt, power, will, endoreality and other key ideas underpinning this work, they are all explored in depth in the *Binding Chaos* series.

I hope you find these books useful in your work!

H.

How To Dismantle a Dictatorship

Heather Marsh

The Binding Chaos Series

The Ontology Quartet
Self – The Creation of Me, Them and Us
Life - Abstracting Divinity
Will – Free Will and Seductive Coercion
Consciousness – Shaping Reality

The Sociology Quartet

Person - The Theft of Self
Power - Great Men, Commoners, Witches and Wretches
Nation – The Fourth Age of Nations
Governance - Autonomy Diversity Society

The Institutions Quartet

Economy – The Power Economy
Law – Law and Chaos
Knowledge – Political Science
Technology - Code Will Rule

The Resistance Series

Stigmergy: How to Create a Mass Movement

Heather Marsh
Stigmergy

How to Create a
Mass Movement

Coming Soon...

How to Combat Coercion
How to Survive the End of Empires
How to Build Community during
Conflict

The Binding Chaos Series

Heather Marsh is a passionate
champion of human rights and the
driving force behind many of the most
influential movements of the past
decades. Her Binding Chaos theory
reveals the principles that guide her
actions and create her tireless
dedication to change.

www.ingramcontent.com/pod-product-compliance
Lightning Source LLC
Chambersburg PA
CBHW052113030426
42335CB00025B/2969